Mata Mata Turtle

Mata Mata Turtles Pet Owner's Guide

Mata Mata Care, Behavior, Diet, Interaction, Costs and Health.

By

Ben Team

I0099090

Published by: Pesa Publishing

Table of Contents

About the Author

The author, Ben Team, is an environmental educator and author with over 16 years of professional reptile-keeping experience.

Ben currently maintains www.FootstepsInTheForest.com, where he shares information, narration and observations of the natural world.

Foreword

As a group, pet lovers like a variety of different types of animals. Some prefer cute-and-cuddly pets, such as dogs, cats and rabbits, while others prefer to care for unusual-looking creatures. This includes everything from hair-covered tarantulas to snake-like fish to fantastically adorned lizards that bear an array of interesting protuberances, crests and spines.

In fact, a number of reptile species clearly fall into the "unusual-looking" category – it is part of what makes them popular with reptile-keeping enthusiasts. But for those who want one of the most unique- and strange-looking creatures in the world, there are few better options than the mata mata turtle.

Mata mata turtles don't look very much like any other turtle species in the world. They are extremely flattened, their face bears a permanent smiling expression and they are covered in various warts, tubercles and flaps, emerging from their head, neck and legs.

Like most other unusual-looking animals, mata matas have evolved to look like they do in response to the evolutionary pressures facing them. Mata matas are ambush-hunting predators of shallow puddles, swamps and ponds, who've evolved to be invisible amid the dark water and leaves in these waters. Their camouflaged appearance isn't only limited to their color pattern; their very shape and body form have also evolved to resemble the habitats in which they live.

All of these factors make mata matas very popular among turtle enthusiasts. But, unfortunately, mata matas are not especially easy to maintain in a captive setting. They have very specific water quality requirements, they grow quite large and most of the individuals on the market were wild-caught, as captive reproduction of the species is quite rare.

But, that doesn't mean you can't successfully maintain one of these remarkable animals. You can have success with mata matas, you just need to learn as much as you can about the animals, so that you can provide them with the type of habitat, food and thermal environment they require.

You can start learning about these amazing animals on the pages that follow. And although you should never view a single source of information as a comprehensive guide, you should be better prepared to care for a mata mata after finishing this volume.

PART I: THE MATA MATA TURTLE

Properly caring for any animal requires an understanding of the species and its place in the natural world. This includes digesting subjects as disparate as anatomy and ecology, diet and geography, and reproduction and physiology.

It is only by learning what your pet is, how it lives, what it does that you can achieve the primary goal of animal husbandry: Providing your pet with the highest quality of life possible.

Chapter 1: Mata Mata Turtle Description and Anatomy

Mata mata turtles (*Chelus fimbriata*) look much different than many other turtles, and they exhibit a number of characteristics that are unique to the species.

The most obvious differences include their flattened shape, unusual face (which appears to feature a smiling expression) and unusual skin, which bears a number of fleshy protuberances.

Yet despite their unique morphology, mata matas possess a typical, bilaterally symmetric vertebrate body plan, including a head, long neck, tail, and four legs.

Size

Although they start life at relatively small sizes, mata matas become quite large by the time they reach maturity. Most hatchlings weigh about ½ ounce (15 grams) and have carapace lengths of about 2 inches (5 centimeters). They grow steadily over the next few years, and ultimately reach carapace lengths of about 16 inches (40 centimeters) and weights of about 33 pounds (15 kilograms).

Some individuals grow slightly larger than this and reach shell lengths of about 18 inches (45 centimeters). Females reach slightly larger sizes than males do.

Color and Pattern

Mata mata turtles are variable in color, but most are primarily brown or gray. Some may have lighter colors, including cream or off-white, and a few possess red markings – particularly under the bottom of the shell. Some hatchling may even be more-or-less completely red. The shell and the body can be similar in color, but some mata matas have shells that are colored differently than their bodies are.

Young mata matas often exhibit more highly contrasting color patterns than older turtles do. Additionally, some mata matas develop a coat of algae on their shells with age.

The overall effect of the mata mata color pattern creates a remarkably well-camouflaged animal, which can be very difficult to see in its natural habitat.

Shell

Mata matas have rigid, flattened shells, which provide them with protection from predators. The shells are roughly oval in shape when viewed from above.

The top portion of a turtle's shell is called the carapace, while the bottom portion is called the plastron. The portions of the shell that connect the carapace to the plastron are called the lateral bridge.

These shells are created from a combination of rib bones and dermal plates (bony plates that originate within the skin). Keratinized plates, called scutes, lie on top of the bony layer.

Interestingly, the plate-like bones outnumber the keratin-based scutes. This means that the margins of the scutes do not occur in the same places that the bones fuse together, which gives additional strength to the shell.

Mata matas have five vertebral (or central) scutes that form a row down the center of the back. Flanking the vertebral scutes are the costal (or pleural) scutes, numbering eight in total (four on each side).

Twenty-four marginal scutes lie around the margin of the carapace (12 on each side). The plastron features six pairs of scutes, termed (moving posteriorly) the gulars, humerals, pectorals, abdominals, femorals and anals. They also – like most of their closest relatives – have a single scute called an intergular, located between the two gular scutes.

Hatchling mata matas have relatively soft, flexible shells. The shell will harden over time, but they remain especially vulnerable to predators until then.

Turtles are firmly attached to their shells; they cannot crawl out of them, as is frequently seen in cartoons and comic strips. Accordingly, a turtle's shell grows along with the turtle.

Legs

Mata matas have relatively muscular legs that are adapted for walking on the bottom of the rivers and ponds they inhabit. Their feet are webbed, but they are not very good swimmers. Most mata matas have five toes on their front feet and four on their rear feet.

Head, Neck and Face

Like all other living turtles, mata matas lack teeth. Instead, they have a bony beak (technically called a rhamphotheca), which is covered by a layer of keratin. The mouths of mata matas are specialized for suction feeding, and they lack the jaw strength of most similar-sized turtles. When viewed from the front, mata matas appear as though they are smiling, thanks to the unique shape of their mouths.

The eyes of mata matas sit on the sides of their heads, although the front of their faces are pointed, which allows them to see in front of their face as well as to the sides. The eyes are usually yellow to brown with a dark stripe passing through the center. The pupil is round.

Mata matas have elongated snorkel-like noses. This allows them to more easily reach the surface while resting on the bottom of shallow ponds and rivers.

Mata mata turtles have tympanums (essentially akin to an ear drum) located behind the corner of the mouth, but you probably won't notice them, unless you look closely.

Note the smiling expression on this mata mata's face.

Tail

Mata matas have relatively short tails. The tails play little to no role in locomotion or defense, but they do serve as the location for the vent, which is important in elimination and reproduction.

Although immature males and females have similar-looking tails, those of mature males are longer and thicker than those of mature females are.

Additionally, the location of the vent on the tail differs in males and females. In females, the vent is located inside the margin of the shell; the vents of males are located more distally, and they lie outside the margin of the vent. This arrangement allows males to breed with the females.

Internal Anatomy

While the average turtle keeper need not understand the internal anatomy of their pet enough to perform exploratory surgery, a basic understanding of the turtle's internal world is necessary.

In most respects, turtles have internal anatomy that is similar to that of other vertebrates, such as humans. Accordingly, special attention is warranted for those aspects that differ from those of most other animals.

Skeletal System

One of the unique aspects of the internal anatomy of turtles is their skeletal system.

As with most other vertebrates, turtles have both axial and appendicular skeletons. The skull, vertebral column and ribs form the axial skeleton, while the shoulder girdle, pelvic girdle and limbs comprise the appendicular skeleton.

However, in turtles, the ribs are fused to the shell. Unlike other vertebrates, whose pelvic and hip girdles are located *outside* the rib cage, turtles carry these bones *inside* their rib cage. While this arrangement helps to protect these areas from damage, it limits the mobility of most turtles.

Digestive System

The digestive system of mata matas is similar to that of other turtles, and, to a lesser extent, vertebrates in general.

Just inside the mouth likes the esophagus, which transports food to the stomach. From here, food passes through the small and then large intestines before being expelled from the vent.

The pancreas and spleen lie close to the stomach, while the gallbladder attaches to the liver, just as it does in most other vertebrates.

Circulatory and Pulmonary System

In general, the circulatory and pulmonary systems of turtles are similar to those of other reptiles.

Turtles inhale and exhale through their mouth or nose, while the trachea carries air to and from two lungs. Because the turtle's shell is rigid, which prevents the ribs from moving (which would pump air into and out of the lungs), turtles have a collection of membranes and connective tissues that attach to the distal ends of the lungs. When these connective tissues contract and relax, the lungs empty and fill with air.

Like many other reptiles, turtles have three-chambered hearts, which feature two atria and a single ventricle. One atrium accepts oxygenated blood from the lungs, while the other atrium receives oxygen-poor blood from the body.

Both atria pump blood into a single ventricle, which then pumps the blood into the rest of the body. Normally, as in many other reptiles, this means that the turtle's body receives a combination of oxygen-rich and oxygen-poor blood. However, turtles have a primitive septum (wall) in their ventricle, which partially prevents the mixing of the two types of blood.

Accordingly, turtles have a slightly more efficient cardiovascular system than lizards and snakes do.

Urinary System

Mata matas filter waste products from their bloodstream via their paired kidneys. They then store these waste products in the urinary bladder. These waste products are released primarily in the form of urea. (Khalil, 1947)

Turtles have a renal portal blood system, which means that the blood traveling through the rear half of the turtles' body is filtered by the kidneys before making it to the front half of the body. This has important implications in turtle medical care; medications cannot be injected into the rear half of the body, as their kidneys will filter the medications before they can circulate widely.

Reproductive System

Turtle fertilization occurs internally, so they must mate to reproduce.

Males have a single intromittent organ (penis), making them similar to crocodilians and birds, but very different from snakes and lizards, who possess paired reproductive organs (termed hemipenes).

The penis of male turtles is held inverted, inside the tail base. During mating attempts, the penis everts and protrudes outside of the vent.

Females have a pair of ovaries, in which eggs form and reside; and a pair of oviducts, which accept the eggs once they are released. The eggs join the sperm inside the oviducts, where they continue to develop.

Before the eggs are deposited, calcium and other minerals coat the surface of the developing embryos, thus giving rise to the eggshell.

Like females of many other species, mata matas can likely retain sperm from a single mating for many months and possibly longer.

Chapter 2: Mata Mata Biology and Behavior

Mata matas are unique turtles, who exhibit a number of biological and behavioral adaptations that allow them to survive in their natural habitats.

Growth

The growth rate of mata matas varies in relation to the amount of food they can acquire. Accordingly, because they benefit from essentially unlimited food, captive mata matas grow much more quickly than their wild counterparts do. In fact, wild mata matas may fail to grow for several years if they are unable to obtain sufficient food.

Like most other reptiles, mata matas grow quickly while they are young, but their growth rate slows considerably once they reach maturity. Mata matas can double their body weight over their first few months of life.

By 5 to 7 years of age, most captive mata matas are approaching maturity, but wild mata matas may take several times as long to reach maturity.

Shedding

Like all other animals, mata matas shed their skin; however, unlike snakes and lizards, who shed all of their scales at the same time, mata matas shed on a rather continual basis. Because they replace very small pieces of skin at a time, the process usually goes unnoticed.

However, sometimes – particularly during periods of rapid growth – mata matas may increase the amount of skin they shed in a short time period, which makes the process more conspicuous. Your pet may ingest his shed skin in an effort to avoid wasting any nutrients.

Lifespan

Most turtles live long lives, and mata matas are no exception. As is the case for most other chelonians, most mortality likely occurs among eggs, hatchlings and juveniles, rather than mature adults. However, things like habitat destruction and disease remain significant threats for the entirety of the turtles' lives.

Unfortunately, the typical lifespan of mata matas is not well known. They likely live for at least 15 to 20 years, and they may live for two or three times this long.

Senses and Intelligence

Mata matas possess the same senses that most other turtles do. They have poor good eyesight, respond to tactile stimulation readily and appear to have a strong sense of smell. They are thought to have very good hearing by turtle standards, which may be an adaptation that helps them to ambush passing fish.

Turtles have a larger brain size index than most lizards and snakes do, but this does not mean they are especially intelligent.

Nevertheless, mata matas can learn to anticipate routine maintenance, and they may even begin to associate their keeper with food. This can lead them to "beg" for food, by repeatedly come toward you as you approach the enclosure.

Metabolism and Digestion

Like most other non-avian reptiles, mata matas have slow metabolisms. This not only means that it takes them longer than many other animals to process their food but also, they require less food to remain alive.

In general, ectothermic ("cold-blooded") animals require about one-fifth to one-twentieth of the food that similarly sized endothermic ("warm-blooded") animal do.

Locomotion

Mata matas are weak swimmers, who primarily get around by walking along the bottom of the ponds and rivers in which they live. This is part of the reason they are partial to very shallow waters. Mata matas spend most of their lives in the water, but they are also capable of moving across dry land.

Diel and Seasonal Behavioral Patterns

Mata matas are primarily nocturnal animals, meaning that they are active during the night and sleep during the day. However, they are adaptable and may be active at any hour of the day or night.

Because mata matas live in tropical regions, which experience relatively little seasonal differences in climate, mata matas do not exhibit many seasonal behavior patterns.

Defensive Strategies

Mata matas try to avoid encounters with predators whenever possible. Their cryptic colors and patterns help to accomplish this goal, as does their habit of inhabiting debris-filled ponds, where visibility is poor.

However, when cornered or unable to escape a predator, they may also bite or scratch at the perceived threat, and some individuals may void the contents of their cloaca when frightened.

Mature mata matas occasionally fall prey terrestrial predators, but humans, crocodilians and jaguars are likely the only serious threats to most individuals.

Hatchling and juvenile mata matas, on the other hand, are vulnerable to a wide variety of predators in their natural habitats. Some of their predators include birds, terrestrial carnivores, large fish, wading birds and snakes.

Foraging

Mata matas are primarily ambush hunters, who wait for fish to approach them. However, they will occasionally chase after fish, and some have been seen corralling fish into areas from which escape is difficult. They can then feed more leisurely.

Chapter 3: Classification and Taxonomy

Scientists place species in a multi-tiered classification scheme to help facilitate communication and to signify the evolutionary relationships among closely related taxa.

Understanding this classification scheme can help you better understand painted turtles and their place in the tree of life.

Reptiles in the Tree of Life

For decades, scientists have debated the definition of the term "reptile." (Anderson, 2003)

On the one hand, lizards, snakes, crocodiles and turtles are all instantly recognizable as reptiles, thanks to their scaly skin and other traits.

However, the reptile evolutionary lineage, when considered in its entirety, must also include dinosaurs, and their direct descendants, the birds.

Regardless of which definition taxonomists ultimately agree upon, the history of the group is relatively well known. Reptiles first evolved approximately 300 million years ago, when they branched off the amphibian family tree.

This lineage produced an amazing array of species, including dinosaurs, mosasaurs and pterodactyls, as well as the ancestors of modern snakes, lizards and turtles. Most of these lineages died out almost completely, but a few managed to survive to the present day. Currently, reptiles are represented by the following groups:

- Crocodilians

- Squamates (snakes and lizards)

- Sphenodontids (tuataras)

- Testudines (turtles)

- Birds

Testudines in the Tree of Life

All living turtles can trace their origin back to the same ancestral species, meaning that all living turtles are part of the same evolutionary lineage. Scientists call such lineages monophyletic.

Two different names are commonly used to refer to the group, including "testudines" and "chelonians". While modern looking turtles likely appeared in the Jurassic period, a few primitive turtle fossils have been discovered from Triassic period deposits.

These turtles, which lived about 220 million years ago, differed greatly from modern turtles. Not only did they lack the proper shell of modern chelonians, they had teeth embedded in their upper and lower jaws.

Because of the unique body plan of testudines (a term that refers to all the various types of turtles, including marine, terrestrial and freshwater species), scientists have long debated the group's placement within the tree of life.

Those swayed by morphological data believe that turtles are most closely aligned with Lepidosaurs (a group that includes snakes, lizards and tuataras). In part, this is based on the holes (fenestra) in the skulls of ancient turtles, which resemble those present in the skulls of lizards and snakes.

However, recent genetic studies of a wide variety of species have shed light on the placement of turtles within the tree of life, as well as the placement of individual species within the turtle umbrella. (Crawford, 2012)

According to this new research, turtles are the sister group to archosaurs (a group that includes crocodilians, birds and several extinct groups, such as non-avian dinosaurs). Lepidosaurs are the sister group to the ancestor of both archosaurs and Testudines (a group named the Archosauria).

This means that the closest living relatives of turtles are crocodilians and birds, rather than snakes and lizards. Nevertheless, the two groups diverged from a common path hundreds of millions of years ago. So, while the two groups are each other's closest living relatives, they are not especially closely related.

As of November 2016, scientists currently recognize 346 living Testudines, but this number fluctuates as new species are discovered, different species are synonymized, and subspecies are elevated to the level of full species.

Mata Matas in the Tree of Life

Herpetologists categorize all living turtles in the order Testudines. The first major division in this lineage occurs between those turtles who withdraw their neck in a lateral plane (called the sub-order Pleurodira), and those who draw their neck back in a vertical plane, called the sub-order Cryptodira.

Mata matas are in the former group, the Pleurodira. There are only three families within the Pleurodira, including the one to which mata matas belong: Chelidae. Most members of the Chelidae live in South America, Australia or southeast Asia.

There are a number of genera within the family Chelidae, including *Chelus*, which contains the mata mata. The mata matas (*Chelus fimbriata*) is the only species in the genus, although some workers have tried to split the species into two or more subspecies.

Chapter 4: The Mata Mata's World

Mata matas are habitat specialists, who tend to inhabit slow-moving streams, stagnant ponds and swamps. However, they can adapt to slightly different conditions when necessary.

Basic Geography

Mata matas are confined to the northern portions of South America. They inhabit portions of Brazil, Bolivia, Peru, Ecuador, Columbia, Suriname, Guyana, French Guyana and Venezuela.

They typically inhabit shallow waters, which are rich in tannins, thanks to the decomposing plant materials present in the water. They generally eschew waters with strong currents.

Climate

Although there are subtle climate differences across the mata mata's range, they essentially experience a humid, tropical climate, which remains warm and damp throughout most of the year.

Rainfall timing varies across the range, but is generally high in all portions of the mata mata's range.

Ecology

Like all other animals, mata matas must interact with other organisms in their habitats – they do not live in a vacuum. Mata matas must live alongside countless other species, drawing resources from some and avoiding threats represented by others. Still other species play no appreciable role in the lives of these unique turtles.

Prey

Mata matas will consume virtually any small creature they can catch and overpower, but fish are clearly the most important prey class for these turtles.

However, they will also consume small invertebrates, and likely the occasional snake, frog or small turtle they encounter.

Predators

From the time they are buried in the ground as eggs until they reach 3 to 5 years of age, mata matas have a variety of predators, representing most common lineages.

Large snakes opportunistically consume small turtles, just like predatory birds and mammals do. Large fish, amphibians and other turtles can also represent a threat.

Once mature, mata matas are safe from all but the largest or most formidable and determined predators, such as canids, felids, crocodilians and humans.

Other Associations

Wild mata matas often suffer from a variety of internal parasites, including roundworms, tapeworms and flagellate protozoans. Leaches often attach themselves to the inside rim of the shells of mata matas.

Although these parasites rarely cause health problems for healthy turtles, stressed, injured, malnourished or diseased specimens may succumb to such infestations.

PART II: MATA MATA HUSBANDRY

Once equipped with a basic understanding of what mata matas *are* (Chapter 1 and Chapter 3), where they *live* (Chapter 4), and what they *do* (Chapter 2) you can begin learning about their captive care.

Animal husbandry is an evolving pursuit. Keepers shift their strategies frequently as they incorporate new information and ideas into their husbandry paradigms.

There are few "right" or "wrong" answers, and what works in one situation may not work in another. Accordingly, you may find that different authorities present different, and sometimes conflicting, information regarding the care of these turtles.

In all cases, you must strive to learn as much as you can about your pet and its natural habitat, so that you may provide it with the best quality of life possible.

Chapter 5: Mata Matas as Pets

Mata matas can make rewarding pets, but you must know what to expect before adding one to your home and family. This includes not only understanding the nature of the care they require, but also the costs associated with this care.

Assuming that you feel confident in your ability to care for a turtle and endure the associated financial burdens, you can begin seeking your individual pet.

Understanding the Commitment

Keeping a mata mata as a pet requires a substantial commitment. You will be responsible for your pet's well-being for the rest of its life. Most turtles are long-live animals, and you must be prepared to care for your new pet for many years.

Can you be sure that you will still want to care for your pet several years in the future? Do you know what your living situation will be? What changes will have occurred in your family? How will your working life have changed over this time?

You must consider all of these possibilities before acquiring a new pet. Failing to do so often leads to apathy, neglect and even resentment, which is not good for you or your pet turtle.

Neglecting your pet is wrong, and in some locations, a criminal offense. You must continue to provide quality care for your mata mata, even once the novelty has worn off, and it is no longer fun to maintain his habitat and feed him each week.

Once you purchase a turtle, its well-being becomes your responsibility until it passes away at the end of a long life, or you have found someone who will agree to adopt the animal for you. Unfortunately, this is rarely an easy task. You may begin with thoughts of selling your pet to help recoup a small part of your investment, but these efforts will largely fall flat.

While professional breeders may profit from the sale of mata matas, amateurs are at a decided disadvantage. Only a tiny sliver of the general population is interested in reptilian pets, and only a small subset of these are interested in keeping mata matas.

Of those who are interested in acquiring a mata mata, most would rather start fresh, by *purchasing* a small hatchling or juvenile from an established breeder, rather than adopting your questionable animal *for free.*

After having difficulty finding a willing party to purchase or adopt your animal, many owners try to donate their pet to a local zoo. Unfortunately, this rarely works either.

Zoos are not interested in your mata mata, no matter how pretty and well-established he is. He is a pet with little to no reliable provenance and questionable health status. This is simply not the type of animal zoos are eager to add to their multi-million-dollar collections.

Zoos obtain most of their animals from other zoos and museums; failing that, they obtain their animals directly from their land of origin. As a rule, they do not accept donated pets.

No matter how difficult it becomes to find a new home for your unwanted turtle, you must never release non-native reptiles into the wild.

Additionally, released or escaped reptiles cause a great deal of distress to those who are frightened by them. This leads local municipalities to adopt pet restrictions or ban reptile keeping entirely.

The Costs of Captivity

Reptiles are often marketed as low-cost pets. While true in a relative sense (the costs associated with dog, cat, horse or tropical fish husbandry are often much higher than they are for mata matas), potential keepers must still prepare for the financial implications of turtle ownership.

Mata matas tend to walk along the bottom, rather than swim.

At the outset, you must budget for the acquisition of your pet, as well as the costs of purchasing or constructing a habitat. Unfortunately, while many keepers plan for these costs, they typically fail to consider the on-going costs, which will quickly eclipse the initial startup costs.

Startup Costs

One surprising fact most new keepers learn is the enclosure and equipment will often cost as much as (or more than) the animal does (except in the case of very high-priced specimens).

Prices fluctuate from one market to the next, but in general, the least you will spend on a healthy mata mata is about $250 (£190), while the least you will spend on the *initial* habitat and assorted equipment will be about $100 (£75). Replacement equipment and food will represent additional (and ongoing) expenses.

Examine the charts on the following pages to get an idea of three different pricing scenarios. While the specific prices listed will vary based on innumerable factors, the charts are instructive for first-time buyers.

The first scenario details a budget-minded keeper, trying to spend as little as possible. The second example estimates the costs for a keeper with a moderate budget, and the third example provides a case study for extravagant shoppers, who want an expensive turtle and top-notch equipment.

These charts are only provided estimates; your experience may vary based on a variety of factors.

Inexpensive Option

Small, Wild-Caught Mata Mata	$250 (£190)
Economy Homemade Habitat	$50 (£38)
Light Fixtures and Bulbs	$50 (£38)
Plants, Substrate, Hides, etc.	$20 (£15)
Water Filter	$50 (£38)
Digital Indoor-Outdoor Thermometer	$20 (£15)
Water Dish, Food Dishes, Spray Bottles, Misc.	$20 (£15)
Total	**$460 (£349)**

Moderate Option

Large, Wild-Caught Mata Mata	$500 (£376)
Premium Homemade Habitat	$150 (£112)
Light Fixtures and Bulbs	$50 (£38)
Plants, Substrate, Hides, etc.	$20 (£16)
Water Filter	$100 (£75)
Digital Indoor-Outdoor Thermometer	$20 (£16)
Water Dish, Food Dishes, Spray Bottles, Misc.	$20 (£16)
Total	**$860 (£649)**

Premium Option

Captive Bred Mata Mata	$1000 (£752)
Premium Commercial Enclosure	$500 (£383)
Light Fixtures and Bulbs	$50 (£38)
Plants, Substrate, Hides, etc.	$20 (£15)
Water Filter	$200 (£150)
Digital Indoor-Outdoor Thermometer	$20 (£15)
Water Dish, Food Dishes, Spray Bottles, Misc.	$20 (£15)
Total	**$1,810 (£1,368)**

Ongoing Costs

The ongoing costs of mata mata ownership primarily fall into one of three categories: food, maintenance and veterinary care.

Food costs are the most significant of the three, but they are relatively consistent and somewhat predictable. Some maintenance costs are easy to calculate, but things like equipment malfunctions are impossible to predict with any certainty. Veterinary expenses are hard to predict and vary wildly from one year to the next.

Food Costs

Food is the single greatest ongoing cost you will experience while caring for your mata mata. To obtain a reasonable estimate of your yearly food costs, you must consider the number of meals you will feed your pet per year and the cost of each meal.

The amount of food your turtle will consume will vary based on numerous factors, including his size, the average temperatures in his habitat and his health.

As a ballpark number, you should figure that you'll need about $10 (£8) per week – roughly $500 (£376) per year -- for food. You could certainly spend more or less than this, but that is a reasonable estimate for back-of-the-envelope calculations.

Veterinary Costs

While you should always seek veterinary advice at the first sign of illness, it is probably not wise to haul your healthy turtle to the vet's office for no reason – they don't require "checkups" or annual vaccinations as some other pets may. Accordingly, you shouldn't incur any veterinary expenses unless your pet falls ill.

However, veterinary care can become very expensive, very quickly. In addition to a basic exam or phone consultation, your turtle may need cultures, x-rays or other diagnostic tests performed. In light of this, wise keepers budget at least $200 to $300 (£160 to £245) each year to cover any emergency veterinary costs.

Maintenance Costs
It is important to plan for both routine and unexpected maintenance costs. Commonly used items, such as paper towels, disinfectant and replacement filter media are rather easy to calculate. However, it is not easy to know how many burned out light bulbs, cracked misting units or faulty thermostats you will have to replace in a given year.

Those who keep their turtle in simple enclosures will find that about $50 (£40) covers their yearly maintenance costs. By contrast, those who maintain elaborate habitats may spend $200 (£160) or more each year.

Always try to purchase frequently used supplies, such as light bulbs, paper towels and disinfectants in bulk to maximize your savings. It is often beneficial to consult with local reptile-keeping clubs, who often pool their resources to attain greater buying power.

Myths and Misunderstandings

Unfortunately, there are many myths and misunderstandings about mata matas and reptile-keeping in general. Some myths represent outdated thinking or techniques, while other myths and misunderstandings reflect the desires of keepers, rather than the reality of the situation.

Myth: *Mata matas will only grow to the size of their enclosure, and then they stop growing entirely.*

Fact: Despite the popularity of this myth, healthy turtles do not stop growing until they reach their final size. Keeping a turtle in a small cage is an inhumane practice that will only lead to a stressed, sick animal.

Myth: *Mata matas are reptiles, so they are not capable of suffering or feeling pain.*

Fact: While it is important to avoid anthropomorphizing, or projecting human emotions and motivations to non-human entities, reptiles – including mata matas – feel pain. There is no doubt that they can experience pain and seek to avoid it. While it is impossible to know exactly what a turtle thinks, there is no reason to believe that they do not suffer similarly to other animals, when injured, ill or depressed.

Myth: *You can feed a mata mata commercial turtle pellets.*

Fact: Although a small number of keepers manage to train their mata mata to feed on turtle pellets or other prepared foods, most will require live fish for their entire lives.

Myth: *My mata mata likes to be held so he can feel the warmth of my hands.*

Fact: In truth, your mata mata may tolerate being held for brief periods, but it probably does not "like" it. This myth springs from the notion that because reptiles are "cold blooded," and they must derive their heat from external sources, they enjoy warmth at all times. In truth, while turtles are ectothermic or "cold blooded," they are most comfortable within a given range of temperatures. This temperature varies with the season and over the course of the day, but averages between about 75 and 85 degrees Fahrenheit (24 to 29 degrees Celsius) – your hands are actually a bit warm for the animals.

Myth: *Turtles never bite because they do not have teeth.*

Fact: While it is true that turtles and tortoises lack teeth, their beaks are often strong, hard and sharp. To be clear: Mata matas are not likely to bite their keepers, but it is a possibility. Their bites are unlikely to cause significant damage, but caution is still warranted.

Myth: *Mata matas are good pets for young children.*

Fact: While many turtles make wonderful pets for adults, teenagers and families, they require more care than a young child can provide. The age at which a child is capable of caring for a turtle will vary, but children should be about ten years of age before they are allowed to care for their own turtle. Parents must exercise prudent judgment and make a sound assessment of their child's capabilities and maturity. Children will certainly enjoy pet turtles, but they must be cared for by someone with adequate maturity. Additionally, it is important to consider the potential for young children contracting salmonella and other pathogens from the family pet.

Myth: *If you get tired of a turtle, it is easy to find a new home for it. The zoo will surely want your pet; after all, you are giving it to them free of charge! If that doesn't work, you can always just release it into the wild.*

Fact: Acquiring a pet turtle is a very big commitment. Most turtles are long-lived animals, who may reach 40 to 50 years of age.

If you ever decide that your turtle no longer fits your family or lifestyle, you may have a tough time finding a suitable home for it. You can attempt to sell the animal, but this is illegal in some places, and often requires a permit or license to do legally.

Zoos and pet stores will be reticent to accept your pet – even at no charge – because they cannot be sure that your pet does not have an illness that could spread through their collections. A zoo may have to spend hundreds or thousands of dollars for the care, housing and veterinary care to accept your pet mata mata, and such things are not taken lightly.

Some people consider releasing the turtle into the wild if no other accommodations can be made, but such acts are destructive, often illegal and usually a death sentence for the turtle. Released mata matas will have very little chance of surviving.

You will likely have to solicit the help of a rescue group or shelter devoted to reptiles in finding a new home for an unwanted turtle.

Acquiring Your Mata Mata

Modern reptile enthusiasts can acquire turtles from a variety of sources, each with a different set of pros and cons.

Pet stores are one of the first places many people see mata matas, and they become the de facto source of pets for many beginning keepers. While they do offer some unique benefits to prospective keepers, pet stores are not always the best place to purchase a turtle; so, consider all of the available options, including breeders and reptile swap meets, before making a purchase.

Pet Stores

Pet stores offer a number of benefits to keepers shopping for mata matas, including convenience: They usually stock all of the equipment your new turtle needs, including cages, heating devices and food items.

Additionally, they offer you the chance to inspect the mata mata up close before purchase. In some cases, you may be able to choose from more than one specimen. Many pet stores provide health guarantees for a short period, which provide some recourse if your new pet turns out to be ill.

However, pet stores are not always the ideal place to purchase your new pet. Pet stores are retail establishments, and as such, you will usually pay more for your new pet than you would from a breeder.

Additionally, pet stores rarely know the pedigree of the animals they sell, and they will rarely know the mata mata's date of birth, or other pertinent information.

Other drawbacks associated with pet stores primarily relate to the staff's inexperience. While some pet stores concentrate on reptiles and may educate their staff about proper turtle care, many others provide incorrect advice to their customers.

It is also worth considering the increased exposure to pathogens that pet store animals endure, given the constant flow of animals through such facilities.

Reptile Expos
Reptile expos offer another option for purchasing turtles. Reptile expos often feature resellers, breeders and retailers in the same room, all selling various types of turtles and other reptiles.

Often, the prices at such events are quite reasonable and you are often able to select from many different turtles. However, if you have a problem, it may be difficult to find the seller after the event is over.

Breeders

Because they usually offer unparalleled information and support to their customers, breeders are generally the best place for most novices to shop for mata matas. Additionally, breeders often know the species well and are better able to help you learn the husbandry techniques necessary for success.

The primary disadvantage of buying from a breeder is that you must often make such purchases from a distance, either by phone or via the internet. Nevertheless, most established breeders are happy to provide you with photographs of the animal you will be purchasing, as well as his or her parents.

Selecting Your Mata Mata

Not all mata matas are created equally, so it is important to select a healthy individual that will give you the best chance of success.

Practically speaking, the most important criterion to consider is the health of the animal. However, the sex, age and history of the turtle are also important things to consider.

Health Checklist

Always check your turtle thoroughly for signs of injury or illness before purchasing it. If you are purchasing the animal from someone in a different part of the country, you must inspect it immediately upon delivery. Notify the seller promptly if the animal exhibits any health problems.

Avoid the temptation to acquire or accept a sick or injured animal in hopes of nursing him back to health. Not only are you likely to incur substantial veterinary costs while treating your new pet, you will likely fail in your attempts to restore the turtle to full health. Sick animals rarely recover in the hands of novices.

Additionally, by purchasing injured or diseased animals, you incentivize poor husbandry on the part of the retailer. If retailers lose money on sick or injured animals, they will take steps to avoid this eventuality, by acquiring healthier stock in the first place, and providing better care for their charges.

As much as is possible, try to observe the following features:

- **Observe the turtle's shell and skin**. It should be free of lacerations and other damage. Pay special attention to those areas that frequently sustain damage, such as the tip of the tail, the toes and the front of the face. A small cut or abrasion may be relatively easy to treat, but significant abrasions and cuts are likely to become infected and require significant treatment.

- **Gently check the turtle's crevices and creases for leeches**. Try to avoid purchasing any animal that has leeches. Additionally, you should avoid purchasing any other animals from this source, as they may harbor parasites as well.

- **Examine the turtle's eyes, ears and nostrils**. The eyes should not be sunken, and they should be free of discharge. The nostrils should be clear and dry – turtles with runny noses or those who blow bubbles are likely to be suffering from a respiratory infection.

- **Gently palpate the animal and ensure no lumps or anomalies are apparent**. Lumps in the muscles or abdominal cavity may indicate parasites, abscesses or tumors.

- **Observe the turtle's demeanor**. Healthy turtles are aware of their environment and react to stimuli. When active, the animal should calmly explore his environment. Avoid lethargic animals, which do not appear alert.

- **Check the turtle's vent**. The vent should be clean and free of smeared feces. Smeared feces can indicate parasites or bacterial infections.

- **Check the turtle's appetite**. If possible, ask the retailer to feed the turtle small minnow. A healthy, suitably warm animal should usually exhibit a strong food drive, although failing to eat is not *necessarily* a bad sign – the turtle may not be hungry.

The Age
Hatchling turtles are very fragile until they reach about one month of age. Before this, they are unlikely to thrive in the hands of beginning keepers.

Accordingly, most beginners should purchase two- or three-month-old juveniles, who have already become well established. Animals of this age tolerate the changes associated with a new home better than very young specimens do. Further, given their larger size, they will better tolerate temperature and humidity extremes than smaller animals will.

The Sex
Unless you are attempting to breed mata matas, you should select a male pet, as females are more likely to suffer from reproduction-related health problems than males are.

Many females will produce and deposit egg clutches upon reaching maturity, whether they are housed with a male or not. While this is not necessarily problematic, novices can easily avoid this unnecessary complication by selecting males as pets.

Quarantine
Because new animals may have illnesses or parasites that could infect the rest of your collection, it is wise to quarantine

all new acquisitions. This means that you should keep any new animal as separated from the rest of your pets as possible. Only once you have ensured that the new animal is healthy should you introduce it to the rest of your collection.

Always tend to quarantined animals last, as this reduces the chances of transmitting pathogens to your healthy animals. Do not wash quarantined water bowls or cage furniture with those belonging to your healthy animals. Whenever possible, use completely separate tools for quarantined animals and those that have been in your collection for some time.

Always be sure to wash your hands thoroughly after handling quarantined animals, their cages or their tools. Particularly careful keepers wear a smock or alternative clothing when handling quarantined animals.

Quarantine new acquisitions for a minimum of 30 days; 60 or 90 days is even better. Many zoos and professional breeders maintain 180- or 360-day-long quarantine periods.

Chapter 6: Providing the Captive Habitat

The first thing that you need to keep a mata mata as a pet is the enclosure – it is the defining characteristic of captivity!

Over the years, keepers have used a wide variety of enclosure types, each of which offers different benefits and drawbacks. Some keepers prefer inexpensive, functional enclosures and place a premium on things like cost, durability and ease of maintenance, while other keepers desire to build the most visually impressive habitat possible. Still others may design an enclosure well suited for captive reproduction.

Similarly, keepers differ on the space requirements of turtles; some find relatively modest cage sizes to be sufficient, while others prefer to provide their turtles with larger accommodations.

Regardless of which side of the spectrum you fall on, you must always provide your pet with an enclosure that is large enough to meet the turtle's basic needs – minimally including sufficient room to establish thermal gradients, permit exercise and allow mental stimulation for the animal.

As you proceed, consider all of the variables facing you and your pet, and design a habitat that best fits your circumstances.

Types of Enclosures

Mata matas are almost entirely aquatic; so, the bulk of their habitat should hold water. Many commercial options are suitable for small mata matas, including aquaria and plastic turtle tubs. You can also repurpose items such as plastic storage boxes, small swimming pools, pond liners and cattle troughs for your turtle's habitat -- virtually any smooth-sided, non-toxic, durable container will work.

However, relatively few commercial options are appropriate for large mata matas. A handful of commercial turtle tubs and aquaria are marketed for "large" turtles, but most keepers will find it necessary to construct a custom enclosure of some kind.

If you live in a pet- and child-free home, you can forgo a lid for the cage, but if small creatures have access to the habitat, a lid is necessary.

Materials for Custom Enclosures

You'll have to think carefully about the materials you use while constructing a custom enclosure. The bulk of the habitat must hold water, so you'll have to ensure it can do so safely.

Glass, plastic and metal are the most common choices for building custom enclosures, although you can also use cement if you prefer. It is also possible to use wood, provided that you seal it well enough to hold water.

Each material has benefits and drawbacks. For example, glass is heavy and fragile, but it provides excellent visibility of your pet. Metal is extremely durable, but this is a material that requires special tools and knowledge to use.

Plastic is relatively durable, inexpensive and light, but it will become scratched over time. This can present challenges with keeping the tank clean, and scratches look terrible in transparent plastics (such as Plexiglas).

Enclosure Size and Layout

In most cases, rectangular cage designs are superior to square or round cage designs. This is because the rectangular layout allows you to create a more effective thermal gradient in a given amount of space than a square or round layout does.

Additionally, rectangular enclosures provide a longer distance that the animal can travel before reaching a barrier, which is likely to promote better health and well-being.

Nevertheless, some keepers have had great success with cages of all shapes and configurations. As long as the turtle's needs are met, any configuration will work. To some extent, you will have to customize the enclosure to suit your home, given the scale of the enclosure.

Mata mata tanks should have a large footprint, but they need not be very deep; they should not be deeper than the turtle's shell length.

A sloped bottom is ideal, especially if there are plateaus at different depths. For example, you may construct a tank with a 4-square-foot area at about 3 feet (90 centimeters) of depth, connected to another, similar area at about 1 foot (30 centimeters) of depth. A sloped bottom should connect the two.

The proper size for a mata mata's enclosure is a subject of great debate. Many authorities present conflicting suggestions. In all cases, suggested cage sizes should be considered the minimum acceptable. Larger cages are almost always better.

Some experienced keepers advocate that enclosure should be five times the turtle's length long, three times the turtle's length wide, and at least two times the turtle's length deep. "Length" in these contexts refers to the length of the turtle's shell when measured in a straight line.

In other words, by this guideline, a 10-inch-long mata mata requires a 50-inch-long, 30-inch-wide, 20-inch deep enclosure. Likewise, a 2-inch-long yearling would require a cage 10-inches-long, 6-inches-wide and 4-inches deep.

Other authorities recommend arbitrary tank sizes. Such keepers typically recommend starting with a 20- to 40-gallon aquarium, and moving up to 100-gallon aquariums upon maturity. However, it is important to understand that the capacity of the tank varies with the layout.

While a low-profile tank that contains 100 gallons of water may be large enough for a small adult, a typical 100-gallon aquarium sold in pet stores has been designed for fish. Accordingly, such tanks have a very small footprint, but greater depth. Such cages are wholly inappropriate for mata matas.

The Zoological Association of America requires turtles to have enclosures with an area equal to at least five times the length of the turtle's shell by two times the turtle's shell width. The pool area should be at least two times the shell length by two times the shell width. Additionally, an area of dry land equal to the size of the turtle's shell is required.

Chapter 7: Water Quality

As with fish, aquatic turtles require clean, healthy water to remain healthy. While most turtles are not as sensitive to water conditions as fish are, poor water quality can lead to health problems.

Proper filtration and periodic water changes will keep most of the relevant water quality parameters within tolerances, but you may need water conditioners and other chemicals to keep the pH correct and to alleviate any chlorine or chloramine in the water.

Important Aspects of Water Quality

Be sure that you address each of the following water quality issues to keep your turtle's tank water clean.

- Chlorine / Chloramine – Chlorine and chloramine are used as antibacterial agents in tap water. You can remove or neutralize both agents with water conditioners sold at pet stores.

- Ammonia / Nitrites / Nitrates – Ammonia levels in the tank will rise over time, as your turtle releases waste into the water. Ammonia is toxic, but fortunately, nitrifying bacteria can convert ammonia into nitrates. Nitrates are also toxic, but different bacteria can convert nitrates into nitrites, which are relatively harmless. The bacteria necessary to complete the process will form naturally on your filter media. However, it is important to monitor the levels of ammonia, nitrates and nitrites to keep the water as healthy as possible; you can do this with a water test kit.

- pH – Mata matas are more sensitive to pH than many other turtles are. They generally prefer slightly acidic water, with a pH of between 5 and 6.

Filtration

Unless you plan to perform water changes several times each week, a high-quality water filter is necessary for painted turtle maintenance.

Modern filters treat the water in three different ways. The first stage in the process, called mechanical filtration, removes the particulate matter from the tank. The second stage uses bacteria living on the filter media to convert ammonia and its derivatives into safer substances – this is called biological filtration. Finally, the water passes through an activated carbon filter, which bonds with most chemicals passing through it. This step is referred to as chemical filtration.

The style of the water filter is not terribly important; some keepers prefer canister-style filters, while others prefer units that hang on the back of the aquarium. Either style will work – the important consideration is the capacity of the filter.

Filters are rated for varying quantities of water. For example, you may see filters rated for 100-gallon aquariums and others rated for 20-gallon aquariums. These ratings work well for aquariums containing fish, but because turtles create a considerable amount of waste, it is wise to select a filter rated for two to three times the size of your turtle's tank. In other words, if your pet lives in a 50-gallon habitat, purchase a filter rated for 100- or 150-gallon aquariums.

You will need to clean the filter unit regularly to keep it working at peak efficiency. Avoid using any chemicals to do so; instead, simply rinse the unit and filter cartridges with water. Be sure to use "dirty" tank water to rinse the biological filter cartridge, as chlorinated water will kill the bacteria.

Water Changes

While your filter will help keep the tank water clean, few models are effective enough to keep the water clean without a little help. This help comes in the form of partial water changes.

To perform a partial water change, begin by preparing enough new water to replace about half of the water in the tank. Treat the water as necessary to remove or neutralize the chlorine or chloramine, and allow it to warm to room temperature. Then, remove and discard approximately half of the water in the tank. Finally, add the new water to the tank to complete the partial water change.

You can use a bucket to bail water from the turtle tank, but a siphon hose will make the project much easier. Complete a partial water change about once every week or two to keep the water clean and reduce the workload for the tank filter.

Chapter 8: Heating the Enclosure

Ectothermic, or "cold-blooded," animals primarily heat their bodies via external sources, such as by basking in the sunlight or sitting on a warm rock.

When they cannot reach suitable temperatures, they cannot digest their food effectively, move as quickly as necessary or perform other behaviors and bodily functions.

This can lead the animal to become ill. Therefore, to maintain any ectothermic animal, such as a mata mata, you must provide an enclosure with suitable temperatures.

Depending upon your local climate and the manner in which you house your turtle, you may need one or more heating devices as well as the necessary monitoring equipment. Additionally, you must arrange the heating equipment in such a way that you provide the captive with a range of temperatures.

Ideal Climate for Mata Matas

Mata matas hail from tropical habitats, so they generally prefer water temperatures in the mid-80s Fahrenheit (about 30 degrees Celsius). They will remain active at temperatures slightly outside this range, but extreme temperatures will cause them to become inactive.

In most situations, mata matas adjust their activity levels to match the climate. However, extended periods of time at suboptimal temperatures can affect their health of cause them to become dormant.

Temperatures can be allowed to drop at night, just as they do in the wild. Turtles housed indoors can usually be allowed to cool to room temperature (high 60s to the low 70s Fahrenheit) overnight, as long as they are allowed to warm up properly in the daytime. However, it can take a long time to alter the temperature of a large quantity of water, so it is generally best to keep the temperatures relatively consistent.

Thermal Gradients

One of the most basic principles of animal husbandry is to provide captives with a range of conditions, from which they can choose which is the most comfortable.

For example, it is wise to provide all captives – particularly reptiles and other ectothermic critters, who modify their temperature behaviorally – with a range of temperatures in their enclosure.

Keepers call this practice establishing a *thermal gradient*. Creating a thermal gradient is fairly simple -- you just need to place the enclosure heat source(s) at one end of the cage. This way, temperatures will gradually fall with increasing distance from the heat source. The end of the tank with the heating devices will offer very warm temperatures, while the other end of the tank will remain relatively cold. Intermediate temperatures found between the ends will allow the animal to adjust and maintain its internal temperature.

Aim for temperatures in the high-80s to low-90s (about 31 degrees Celsius) directly under or over the heating source, and try to maintain temperatures in the high-70s to low-80s (about 27 to 28 degrees Celsius).

It is not as easy to establish a thermal gradient in an aquatic tank as it is a terrestrial tank, but it is possible. Fortunately, mata matas don't require a thermal gradient as much as many other reptiles do, and they'll usually thrive in a tank of uniform temperatures, if need be.

Heating Devices

You can use any of several different types of heating devices to maintain proper temperatures in your mata mata's enclosure. All have different pros and cons, which make a given device work in one scenario but not another.

Because mata mata enclosures are largely comprised of water, it can be tricky to maintain the proper temperature range and achieve a good thermal gradient. Accordingly, experimentation is often necessary.

CAUTION: Always use care when arranging and operating heating devices and follow all of the manufacturer's instructions.

Heat Lamps

Heat lamps are the most common type of heating device used by turtle keepers to provide basking spots.

When reptile keepers refer to a "heat lamp", they mean a portable light socket surrounded by a shroud. A variety of different bulbs can be screwed into the receptacle. For example, some keepers prefer to use regular, incandescent light bulbs, while others prefer mercury vapor bulbs.

It is easy to adjust the temperature underneath a heat lamp by either changing the distance between the light and the substrate or swapping out the bulb for a different wattage.

Ceramic Heat Emitters

Ceramic heat emitters are used in place of a light bulb in a heat lamp fixture. However, unlike a light bulb, ceramic heat emitters produce no light. They only produce heat, which emanates from the ceramic.

On the plus side, most manufacturers claim that ceramic heat emitters are much more efficient than light bulbs. Additionally, as they produce no light, they can be used to heat the enclosure at night, without disturbing your pet's circadian rhythms.

However, ceramic heat emitters also have negative characteristics. Because they produce no light, you cannot tell if it is on or not by looking at it. This can lead to injuries if you accidentally touch it while it is on.

Ceramic heat emitters are also rather expensive, although when the efficiency and lifespan of the device is taken into consideration, this difference may become insignificant.

Heat Tape
Heat tape is plastic-covered electrical wire that is designed to heat up when current is applied. Heat tape is not appropriate for creating a basking spot, but it may help to keep indoor enclosures at the desired level, when placed underneath the habitat. However, you must be sure to allow air to flow across the heat tape to prevent a dangerous buildup of heat.

Heat tape is largely inappropriate for beginning reptile keepers, as it must be wired by hand. You must use heat tape with a thermostat or rheostat to maintain the proper temperatures. If you do not, the heat tape will become much too hot and may cause a fire.

Care must be used when laying out heat tape, as improper placement can represent a fire hazard – always follow the manufacturer's instructions when assembling or using heat tape.

Heat Pads
Heating pads made for reptiles are generally constructed by enclosing a length of pre-wired heat tape in a plastic cover. Like heat tape, heat pads are not helpful for maintaining a basking spot, but they may help heat the substrate if placed

below the cage. Be sure that the manufacturer's instructions permit this type of use before using a heat pad in this manner.

Heating pads should always be used with a thermostat or rheostat to maintain appropriate temperatures.

Aquarium Heaters

Submersible aquarium heaters can be used to heat a mata mata's tank, but they must be shielded from the turtle to prevent injuries.

However, these types of heaters are not very effective for creating a thermal gradient, so you'll probably still want to use another type of heat source to help create one. Additionally, many aquarium heaters are unable to heat a large tank sufficiently, so you'll want to avoid budget-priced heaters.

Radiant Heat Panels

Radiant heat panels are similar to heating pads, except that they are designed to project heat rather than warm things that are in contact with the device. Additionally, radiant heat panels are usually placed on the ceiling or wall of an enclosure. This makes them very helpful for providing a basking spot.

Radiant heat panels often cost more than heat lamps do, but they provide safer, more controlled heat. However, radiant heat panels must be used with a thermostat to ensure they do not overheat.

Monitoring and Control Equipment

Maintaining an appropriate climate in your pet's enclosure often requires some trial and error, but this does not mean that you should blindly approach the task.

Instead, you must measure the tank temperatures, to ensure they are within the comfortable range for your pet.

Thermometers

Turtle keepers need two different types of thermometers to monitor their pet's environment properly: one to measure the water temperatures and another to measure the surface temperatures of objects in the habitat.

Several different types of thermometers are appropriate for measuring the ambient air temperature, including analog and digital varieties. Often, digital, indoor-outdoor models are the best choice, as they feature a remote sensing probe. These probes allow you to monitor the temperature in two different portions of the habitat simultaneously, such as the basking spot and the burrow.

To measure the surface temperatures in the enclosure – such as the basking spot or the top of your pet's shell while he is under the basking spot – use an infrared, non-contact thermometer. Dedicated keepers often find these tools immensely valuable; invest in a quality unit, as you are likely to end up using it quite often.

Avoid the plastic, "stick-on" variety of thermometer often sold in pet stores.

Rheostats

Rheostats are akin to "volume controls" for heating devices. They work like lamp dimmer switches, as they reduce the amount of electricity reaching the heating device. This reduction in electricity reduces the amount of heat produced by the device.

Rheostats are helpful tools as they allow you to fine-tune the amount of heat supplied by a given device. However, you must still monitor the temperatures regularly, to ensure the cage temperatures stay within the desired range.

Thermostats

Thermostats are similar to rheostats, but they automatically adjust the amount of electricity reaching the heating device, in order to maintain a pre-selected temperature. Several different types of thermostats are available commercially.

Some work by simply switching the power to the heating device on and off. Others work by continually adjusting the amount of electricity reaching the device.

The former are called on-off thermostats while the later are termed pulse-proportional thermostats. On-off thermostats are only suitable for use with heat pads, radiant heat panels or heat tape.

While you must regularly check to ensure your thermostats are working, they are very helpful for maintaining proper cage temperatures, and they largely automate climate control.

Some thermostats feature a night-drop function, which allows you to program the unit to drop the temperatures by a preselected amount each night.

Thermostat Failure

Eventually, all thermostats will fail. Whether this occurs a week after you purchase the unit or 30 years from now remains to be seen, but you must prepare for the possibility.

In a worst-case scenario, thermostat failure can lead to the death of your animals.

You can provide yourself with some protection from thermostat failure by purchasing a high-quality unit, crafted from quality components. However, even expensive thermostats can fail.

Another option is to use two thermostats, wired in series. To accomplish this, you must set the primary thermostat to the preferred temperature range for your animal. You then attach a second thermostat behind the first. Set this thermostat to a few degrees higher than the primary thermostat.

This way, when the primary thermostat fails, the secondary thermostat will allow the temperature to rise a few degrees, but will prevent the habitat from becoming dangerously warm.

Nighttime Heating

If the nighttime temperatures in your home do not fall lower than the low-70s Fahrenheit (approximately 22 degrees Celsius), you can probably avoid providing any form of heat during the nights.

Mata matas generally prefer rather low light levels.

However, if nighttime heating is required, it is important to use heating devices that do not produce bright light, as this would upset your animal's day-night cycles. Instead, try to use heating pads, ceramic heat emitters or radiant heat panels to maintain suitably warm temperatures.

You can use red incandescent bulbs if need be, but these will still provide some light. The degree to which the turtles can see this light is not clear, but the dim light is certainly better than that produced by typical, "white" lights.

Differing Thermal Requirements

Like most other types of animals, small turtles are less tolerant of temperature extremes than large turtles are. In addition, because they have greater surface-to-volume ratios than larger turtles do, small individuals change temperatures much more quickly than their larger counterparts do.

Accordingly, it is wise to keep the maximum temperatures available to small turtles a few degrees below that provided to large individuals, and to keep the minimum temperatures a few degrees higher than those that are provided to large turtles.

Chapter 9: Lighting the Enclosure

Most turtles have very specific lighting needs; deprived of proper lighting, they can develop a variety of behavioral and health problems. However, the specific lighting requirements of mata matas are not well understood.

Because they typically live in the relatively dim light found under the forest canopy, mata matas probably do not require the type of light intensity that many other turtles do.

Accordingly, it is probably wisest to provide mata matas with a variety of light intensities and of different spectrums in their habitats. This way, your turtle can choose the type of light levels are best.

But to provide your turtle with proper lighting, you'll have to understand a few basic things about light.

The Electromagnetic Spectrum

Light is a type of energy that physicists call electromagnetic radiation; it travels in waves. These waves may differ in amplitude, which correlates to the vertical distance between consecutive wave crests and troughs, frequency, which correlates with the number of crests per unit of time, and wavelength.

Wavelength is the distance from one crest to the next, or one trough to the next. Wavelength and frequency are inversely proportional, meaning that as the wavelength increases, the frequency decreases. It is more common for reptile keepers to discuss wavelengths rather than frequencies.

The sun produces energy (light) with a very wide range of constituent wavelengths. Some of these wavelengths fall within a range called the visible spectrum; humans can detect these rays with their eyes. Such waves have wavelengths between about 390 and 700 nanometers. Rays with wavelengths longer or shorter than these limits are broken into their own groups and given different names.

Those rays with around 390 nanometer wavelengths or less are called ultraviolet rays or UV rays. UV rays are broken down into three different categories, just as the different colors correspond with different wavelengths of visible light. UVA rays have wavelengths between 315 to 400 nanometers, while UVB rays have wavelengths between 280 and 315 nanometers while UVC rays have wavelengths between 100 and 280 nanometers.

Rays with wavelengths of less than 280 nanometers are called x-rays and gamma rays. At the other end of the spectrum, infrared rays have wavelengths longer than 700 nanometers; microwaves and radio waves are even longer.

UVA rays are important for food recognition, appetite, activity and eliciting natural behaviors. UVB rays are necessary for many reptiles to produce vitamin D3. Without this vitamin, reptiles cannot properly metabolize their calcium.

Light Color

The light that comes from the sun and light bulbs is composed of a combination of wavelengths, which create the blended white light that you perceive. This combination of wavelengths varies slightly from one light source to the next.

The sun produces very balanced white light, while "economy" incandescent bulbs produce relatively fewer blue rays and yields a yellow-looking light. High-quality bulbs designed for reptiles often produce very balanced, white light. The degree to which light causes objects to look as they would under sunlight is called the Color Rendering Index, or CRI. Sunlight has a CRI of 100, while quality bulbs have CRIs of 80 to 90; by contrast, a typical incandescent bulb has a CRI of 40 to 50

Light Brightness

Another important characteristic of light that relates to turtles is luminosity, or the brightness of light. Measured in units called Lux, luminosity is an important consideration for your lighting system. While you cannot possibly replicate the intensity of the sun's light, it is desirable in most circumstances to ensure the habitat is lit as well as is reasonably possible.

Without access to appropriately bright lighting, many reptiles become lethargic, depressed or exhibit hibernating behaviors. Dim lighting may inhibit feeding and cause turtles to become stressed and ill.

However, while it is important to provide very bright lighting in portions of the cage, you must also provide the turtles with shade, into which they can retreat if they desire.

Your Turtle's Lighting Needs

To reiterate, mata matas probably require:

- Light that is comprised of visible light, as well as UVA and UVB wavelengths

- Light with a high color-rendering index

- Light of relatively low intensity

Now that you know what your turtle requires, you can go about designing the lighting system for his habitat. Ultraviolet radiation is the most difficult component of proper lighting to provide, so it makes sense to begin by examining the types of bulbs that produce UV radiation.

The only commercially produced bulbs that produce significant amounts of UVA and UVB and suitable for a turtle habitat are linear fluorescent light bulbs, compact fluorescent light bulbs and mercury vapor bulbs.

Neither type of fluorescent bulb produces significant amounts of heat, but mercury vapor bulbs produce a lot of heat and serve a dual function. In many cases, keepers elect to use both types of lights – a mercury vapor bulb for a warm basking site with high levels of UV radiation and fluorescent bulbs to light the rest of the cage without raising the temperature. You can also use fluorescent bulbs to provide the requisite UV radiation and use a regular incandescent bulb to generate the basking spot.

Fluorescent bulbs have a much longer history of use than mercury vapor bulbs, which makes some keepers more comfortable using them. However, many models only produce moderate amounts of UVB radiation. While some mercury vapor bulbs produce significant quantities of UVB, some question the wisdom of producing more UV radiation than the animal receives in the wild. Additionally, mercury vapor bulbs are much too powerful to use in small habitats, and they are more expensive initially.

Most fluorescent bulbs must be placed within 12 inches (25 centimeters) of the basking surface, while some mercury vapor bulbs should be placed farther away from the basking surface – be sure to read the manufacturer's instructions before use. Be sure that the bulbs you purchase specifically state the amount of UVB radiation they produce; this figure is expressed as a percentage, for example 7% UVB. Most UVB-producing bulbs require replacement every six to 12 months – whether or not they have stopped producing light.

However, ultraviolet radiation is only one of the characteristics that turtle keepers must consider. The light bulbs used must also produce a sunlight-like spectrum. Fortunately, most high-quality light bulbs that produce significant amounts of UVA and UVB radiation also feature a high color-rendering index. The higher the CRI, the better, but any bulbs with a CRI of 90 or above will work well. If you are having trouble deciding between two otherwise evenly matched bulbs, select the one with the higher CRI value.

Brightness is the final, and easiest, consideration for the keeper to address. While no one yet knows what the ideal luminosity for a mata mata's enclosure is, it makes sense to ensure that some part of the cage features moderately bright lighting. However, the bulk of the cage should be relatively dim, and offer plenty of protection from the UV-producing lights over the tank. This way, your pet can avoid the light if need be.

Connect the lights to an electric timer to keep the length of the day and night consistent. Most mata matas thrive with 12 hours of daylight and 12 hours of darkness all year long.

Chapter 10: Substrate, Furniture and Plants
Now that you have decided what type of enclosure is right for you and your turtle, you can start placing the necessary items in the tank.

Most reptiles feel more secure in complex habitats than they do barren boxes with no visual barriers or items to investigate. However, you must strike a delicate balance between adding enough items to the enclosure to give your pet a sense of security and overcrowding the habitat, which makes maintenance more difficult and reduces the effective space available to your pet.

Substrates

There are a variety of different substrates you can use for mata mata maintenance. Each has its own set of strengths and weaknesses, so as with every other aspect of husbandry, you'll have to decide which aspects are most important to you when making a decision.

Sands designed specifically for aquarium use are quite effective, and the help provide a natural look. Just be sure that you don't use play sand, as it may cause algae blooms. However, your mata mata may suck in sand particles while feeding, which could lead to impaction. Some keepers prefer very fine sand (which will pass through the turtle's system the easiest), however, others prefer using coarser sands, which are not as likely to be sucked up or carried by gentle currents.

Other keepers use gravel as a substrate. Gravel substrate provides anchoring opportunities for plants, and it looks quite attractive. However, it is possible for your turtle to swallow the rocks, which can lead to health problems. To address this concern, you can use gravel large enough that your turtle cannot ingest it. Be sure to use smooth gravel, as this will help prevent shell injuries.

Gravel substrates often keep the water looking cleaner, as debris tends to settle into the spaces between the small rocks, but this is misleading. While the debris does drift to the bottom of the tank, it still decomposes, releasing water-polluting compounds.

Once trapped in the gravel, this debris is not filtered out of the water. Eventually this requires the keeper to stir up the gravel and perform significant water changes to restore the water quality.

Some keepers prefer using peat as a substrate. Peat is soft and usually settles down to the bottom of the tank well, and it also helps reduce the pH of the tank. This is often helpful for maintaining a good water quality for your turtle.

Still other keepers elect to keep their mata matas in bare-bottomed tanks, with no substrate. While this is rarely as aesthetically pleasing as a gravel or sand substrate, it keeps the water much cleaner, which is more important to your turtle than the visual impact of the habitat.

In all cases, the bottom must be non-abrasive, so that your turtle does not suffer damage to its shell. If you use a cement pond, you will need to cover the bottom with sand or gravel to avoid such problems.

Furniture

Unlike many other commonly kept turtle species, mata matas don't bask very much, if at all. Typically, they spend their lives walking and resting on the bottom of their pond, puddle or swamp, and they only emerge when forced out by competitors, or forced to change ponds to find enough food. Additionally, females leave the water to deposit eggs.

Accordingly, a basking platform is not necessary for mata matas (although females must always be provided with a place that they can get out of the water and deposit eggs).

You can, however, add pieces of drift wood or cork bark to the habitat to help provide the turtle with visual barriers and hiding places. Just be sure that you don't overcrowd the habitat. Also, be sure to anchor any pieces of heavy wood securely, so that they don't topple over on your pet and cause injuries.

Plants

Plants are another great addition to a mata mata enclosure. In addition to providing hiding places for your turtle, plants also compete with algae for nutrients, which can help to reduce algae blooms.

Some keepers prefer to use artificial plants rather than live plants, as they require less care and frequent replacement. These obviously won't alter the water chemistry much, but they'll still provide hiding places and aesthetic appeal.

Because mata matas are strict carnivores, you do not have to worry about the edibility of any plants in the enclosure. However, you will want to select very hardy aquarium plants, as mata matas are likely to destroy fragile species in short order, while moving through the tank.

Chapter 11: Maintaining the Captive Habitat

Now that you have acquired your turtle and set up the enclosure, you must develop a protocol for maintaining his habitat. While turtle habitats require major maintenance every month or so, they only require minor daily maintenance.

In addition to designing a husbandry protocol, you must embrace a record-keeping system to track your turtle's growth and health.

Cleaning and Maintenance Procedures

Once you have decided on the proper enclosure for your pet, you must keep it in proper working order and at the proper temperature level to keep your captive healthy and comfortable. You'll also need to ensure the water quality and chemistry remain suitable.

Some tasks must be completed each day, while others are should be performed weekly, monthly or annually.

Daily

- Monitor the water temperatures of the habitat.

- Spot clean the tank to remove any debris, dead animals, scutes or other items in the water.

- Ensure that the lights, latches and other moving parts are in working order.

- Verify that your turtle is acting normally and appears healthy. You do not necessarily need to handle him to do so.

- Feed your turtle a few minnows, if you are not using an ad libitum feeding model (note that some keepers only feed their captives three or four times per week).

Weekly

- Siphon-clean the tank bottom.

- Clean the inside surfaces of the enclosure.

- Inspect your turtle closely for any signs of injury, parasites or illness.

- Wash and sterilize all tools (tongs, etc.).

- Perform a 25 percent water change.

Monthly

- Conduct a 50 to 75 percent water change.

- Measure and weigh your turtle.

- Photograph your pet (recommended, but not imperative).

- Prune or replace any plants as necessary.

Annually

- Replace the batteries in your thermometers and any other devices that use them.

- Replace UVB lights (some require replacement every six months)

Cleaning your turtle's cage and furniture is relatively simple. Regardless of the way it became soiled, the basic process remains the same:

1. Rinse the object
2. Using a scrub brush or sponge and soapy water, remove any organic debris from the object.
3. Rinse the object thoroughly.
4. Disinfect the object.
5. Re-rinse the object.
6. Dry the object.

Chemicals & Tools

A variety of chemicals and tools are necessary for reptile care. Save yourself some time by purchasing dedicated cleaning products and keeping them together with your tools.

Small Brooms

Small brooms are great for sweeping up small messes and bits of substrate. It is usually helpful to select one that features angled bristles, as they'll allow you to better reach the nooks and crannies of your pet's cage and the surrounding area.

Ideally, the broom should come with its own dust pan to collect debris, but there are plenty of work-arounds for those that don't come with their own.

Scrub Brushes or Sponges

It helps to have a few different types of scrub brushes and sponges on hand for scrubbing and cleaning different items. Use the least abrasive sponge or brush suitable for the task to prevent wearing out cage items prematurely. Do not use abrasive materials on glass or acrylic surfaces. Steel-bristled brushes work well for scrubbing coarse, wooden items, such as branches.

Spatulas and Putty Knives

Spatulas, putty knives and similar tools are often helpful for cleaning reptile cages. They often let you avoid using harsh chemicals, and allow you to simply scrape away stubborn contaminants.

Small Vacuums

Small, handheld vacuums are very helpful for sucking up the dust left behind from substrates. They are also helpful for cleaning the cracks and crevices around the cage doors. A wet-dry shop vacuum, with suitable hoses and attachments, can also be especially helpful, if you have enough room to store it.

Steam Cleaners

Steam cleaners are very effective for sterilizing cages, water bowls and durable cage props after they have been cleaned. In fact, steam is often a better choice than chemical disinfectants, as it will not leave behind a toxic residue. Never use a steam cleaner near your turtle, the plants in his habitat or any other living organisms.

Soap

Use a gentle, non-scented dish soap. Antibacterial soap is preferred, but not necessary. Most people use far more soap than is necessary -- a few drops mixed with a quantity of water is usually sufficient to help remove surface pollutants.

Bleach

Bleach (diluted to one-half cup per gallon of water) makes an excellent disinfectant. Be careful not to spill any on clothing, carpets or furniture, as it is likely to discolor the objects.

Always be sure to rinse objects thoroughly after using bleach and be sure that you cannot detect any residual odor. Bleach does not work as a disinfectant when in contact with organic substances; accordingly, items must be cleaned before you can disinfect them.

Veterinarian Approved Disinfectant

Many commercial products are available that are designed to be safe for their pets. Consult with your veterinarian about the best product for your situation, its method of use and its proper dilution.

Avoid Phenols

Always avoid cleaners that contain phenols, as they are extremely toxic to some reptiles. In general, do not use household cleaning products to avoid exposing your pet to toxic chemicals.

Keeping Records

It is important to keep records regarding your pet's health, growth and feeding, as well as any other important details. In the past, reptile keepers would do so on small index cards or in a notebook. In the modern world, technological solutions may be easier.

You can record as much information about your pet as you like, and the more information to you record, the better. But minimally, you should record the following:

Pedigree and Origin Information

Be sure to record the source of your turtle, the date on which you acquired him and any other data that is available. Breeders will often provide customers with information regarding the sire, dam, date of birth, weights and feeding records, but other sources will rarely offer comparable data.

Feeding Information

Record the date of each feeding, as well as the type of food item(s) offered. It is also helpful to record any preferences you may observe or any meals that are refused.

Weights and Length

Because you look at your pet frequently, it is difficult to appreciate how quickly he is (or isn't) growing. Accordingly, it is important to track his size diligently.

Weigh your turtle with a high quality digital scale. It is often easiest to use a dedicated "weighing container" with a known weight to measure your pet. Simply subtract the weight of the container to obtain the weight of your turtle.

You can measure your turtle's length as well, but it is not as important as his weight.

Maintenance Information

Record all of the noteworthy events associated with your pet's care. This includes anytime you purchase new equipment, supplies or caging. This not only helps to remind you when you purchased the items, but it may help you track down a source for the items in the future, if necessary.

Breeding Information

If you intend to breed your turtles, you should record all details associated with pre-breeding conditioning, cycling, introductions, matings, and egg deposition.

Record all pertinent information about any resulting clutches as well, including the number of viable eggs, as well as the number of unhatched and unfertilized eggs.

Additionally, if you keep several turtles together in the same enclosure, you'll want to be careful to document the details of egg deposition, so you can be sure you know the correct parentage of each egg.

Record Keeping Samples

The following are two different examples of suitable recording systems.

The first example is reminiscent of the style employed by many with large collections. Because such keepers often have numerous animals, the notes are very simple.

The second example demonstrates a simple approach that is employed by many with small collections (or a single pet): keeping notes on paper.

Such notes could be taken in a notebook or journal, or you could type directly into a word processor. It does not matter *how* you keep records, just that you *do* keep records.

Number:	44522	Genus: Chelus Species: fimbriatus	Gender: DOB:	Male 3/20/14	CARD #2
6.30.15 1 dozen minnows	7.08.15 1 dozen minnows	7.14.15 1 dozen minnows	7.21.15 4 worms	7.28.15 1 dozen minnows	
7.02.15 1 dozen minnows	7.10.15 3 worms	7.18.15 1 dozen minnows	7.22.15 50% water change	7.29.15 Changed UVB light	
7.05.15 1 dozen minnows	7.12.15 1 dozen minnows	7.20.15 Weight: 485 grams	7.24.15 1 dozen minnows		

Date	Notes
4-26-13	Acquired "Snorkle" from a breeder named Mark at the in-town reptile expo. Mark explained that Lola's scientific name is Chelus fimbriatus She cost $450. Mark said he purchased the turtle in March, but he does not know the exact date.
4-27-13	Snorkle spent the night in the container I bought her in. I purchased a small plastic storage box cage, a heat lamp and a thermometer at the hardware store, and I ordered a non-contact thermometer, a cannister filter and

	a full-spectrum light online.
4-28-13	Snorkle eagerly ate about 8 minnows that I put in her tank. It was really neat to watch her eat. I can't tell if she's still hungry or not though.
4-29-13	I fed Snorkle another half-dozen minnows, which she ate greedily. She's really good at catching them! But there always seem to be one or two that she can't catch.
5-02-13	Snorkle ate another half-dozen minnows today. I did a 50% water change after she ate.

Chapter 12: Feeding Mata Matas

Feeding your mata mata a healthy diet is one of the most important aspects of his care. This not only means providing your pet with suitable food items, but providing them in the proper way, in the appropriate amounts and on a proper schedule.

Fortunately, mata matas are often easy to feed, and they present few difficulties for their keepers in this respect.

Feeding Your Mata Mata

Mata matas are exclusively carnivorous, and they primarily subsist on fish. However, they'll also consume invertebrates, frogs and other small creatures from time to time.

Accordingly, small fish should form the bulk of your mata mata's diet. You can mix in a few earthworms or shrimp from time to time, if you like; but this is not necessary, and many keepers feel that this is an unnecessary complication.

Most mata matas require live food, although some keepers have had success by holding dead fish with a pair of tongs and "animating" the fish to make them appear alive.

Typically, the easiest way to feed a mata mata is by simply adding a dozen or two fish into the enclosure, and allowing the turtle to dine at his leisure. However, other keepers prefer to offer food at discrete intervals.

As the number of fish swimming in the water decreases, you should add more. This will ensure sufficient prey density to allow your turtle to capture food easily.

Some of the best feeder fish for mata matas include:

- Platies

- Mollies

- Shiners

- Fathead minnows

- Guppies

- Sunfish

- Small sunfish

- Goldfish (Note that goldfish are often highly parasitized, so many keepers like to avoid them).

In general, any small fish species that is not toxic or equipped with sharp or venomous spines. Slow-swimming species are easier for your turtle to catch, but because of their suction-based feeding tactics, mata matas can usually catch most fish, provided that the habitat isn't too large, and the prey is suitably dense.

Because mata matas are often fed on an ad libitum basis, it isn't easy to establish the proper amount of food they require or how often they require it. Accordingly, the best way to proceed is by monitoring your pet's body weight and growth.

Young mata matas should grow consistently if fed the proper amount of food, while adults should maintain a fairly consistent body weight. Adjust the amount of food or the frequency with which you provide it to help keep your turtle appropriately fed.

Vitamin and Mineral Supplements

Many keepers add commercially produced vitamin and mineral supplements to their pet's food on a regular basis. In theory, these supplements help to correct dietary deficiencies and ensure that captive turtles get a balanced diet. In practice, things are not this simple.

The first problem with providing vitamin and mineral supplements to mata matas is that they typically require live food, and the water would wash off any supplement added.

Accordingly, few keepers provide supplements to their turtle as a matter of practice. Instead, they simply try to provide the highest-quality prey possible, in an effort to avoid deficiencies.

Speak with your veterinarian about your turtle's need for vitamin and mineral supplementation, and the best way to provide these items, if necessary.

Chapter 13: Interacting with Your Turtle

You must be sure that your interactions with your turtle are safe and positive for all parties involved. Contact with a large predator (such as yourself) may cause the turtle stress, which can lead to illness and maladaptation. Additionally, improper handling can cause your pet to suffer injuries.

In general, this means that you should avoid most unnecessary physical contact with your pet. This is especially true with mata matas, as they are a shy species, which does not respond to handling very well.

However, you need to observe your turtle for signs of illness regularly, and this will occasionally necessitate directly handling or manipulating the animal.

While it is relatively easy to handle a small mata mata, handling a large adult requires a bit more care. Not only are large individuals heavier than small ones, they may wiggle about while you are holding them, potentially causing you to drop your turtle. Even falls from only a few inches off the ground can cause serious injuries, so you must use great care when lifting your pet.

Handling Your Turtle

Different techniques are necessary for handling turtles of different sizes. Hatchlings are relatively easy to hold, but large adults require entirely different techniques.

Suspending a turtle by its tail can lead to spinal injuries; never use a turtle's tail to support its bodyweight, regardless of its size.

The best way to hold these very small turtles is by placing your index finger on top of the animal's carapace and placing your thumb under its plastron. Do not pinch the shell too firmly, as young turtle shells lack the rigidity of adult shells.

Larger mata matas require two hands to keep their body supported. Place the thumb of each hand on the top or sides of the turtle's carapace, and place the remaining fingers on the turtle's plastron, between the front and back legs.

Transporting Your Pet

From time to time, it will be necessary to transport your pet. When doing so, you must keep the turtle protected from injury, within the appropriate temperature range and protected from sources of stress.

The best way to do so is by placing your turtle in a large plastic storage box, filled with a soft layer of newspaper or hay. Do not fill the container with water when transporting your turtle; however, if your journey will take more than 24 hours or so, be sure to allow the turtle to soak for a few minutes periodically to avoid dehydration.

Opaque boxes will keep your turtle calmer, while transparent boxes will allow you to observe the animal without opening the lid.

Be sure to drill a few ventilation holes on each of the container's vertical sides so that your pet can breathe easily. When drilling the holes, drill from the inside of the tub toward the outside, to prevent any sharp edges from contacting your turtle.

Hygiene

Turtles often carry various strains of *Salmonella* bacteria, as well as other harmful pathogens. While these bacteria rarely cause illness in the turtles, they can make humans – particularly those with compromised immune systems – very ill. In tragic cases, death can result from such infections.

Accordingly, it is imperative to employ sound hygiene practices when caring for a pet turtle. In general, this means:

- Always wash your hands with soap and warm water following any contact with your pet, the enclosure or items that have contacted either.

- Never wash turtle cages, furniture or tools in sinks or bathtubs used by humans.

- Never perform any husbandry tasks in kitchens or bathrooms used by humans.

- Keep high-risk individuals, such as those who are less than 5 years of age, elderly, pregnant or otherwise immunocompromised, away from captive turtles and their habitats.

Chapter 14: Common Health Concerns

Like many other turtles, mata matas are rather hardy animals, but they often suffer from illnesses and injuries that arose during the importation process or once in the keeper's care. Most illnesses occurring after the turtle is in a keeper's care result from improper husbandry, and are therefore, entirely avoidable.

Nevertheless, like most other reptiles, mata matas often fail to exhibit any symptoms that they are sick until they have reached an advanced state of illness. This means that prompt action is necessary at the first hint of a problem. Doing so provides your pet with the greatest chance of recovery.

While proper husbandry is solely in the domain of the keeper, and some minor injuries or illnesses can be treated at home, veterinary care is necessary for many health problems.

Finding a Suitable Vet

While any veterinarian – even one who specializes in dogs and cats – may be able to help you keep your pet happy, it is wise to find a veterinarian who specializes in treating reptiles. Such veterinarians are more likely to be familiar with your pet species and be familiar with the most current treatment standards for reptiles.

Some of the best places to begin your search for a reptile-oriented veterinarian include:

- Veterinary associations

- Local pet stores

- Local colleges and universities

It is always wise to develop a relationship with a qualified veterinarian before you need his or her services. This way, you will already know where to go in the event of an emergency, and your veterinarian will have developed some familiarity with your pet.

When to See the Vet

Most conscientious keepers will not hesitate to seek veterinary attention on behalf of their pet. However, veterinary care can be expensive for the keeper and stressful for the kept, so unnecessary visits are best avoided.

If you are in doubt, call or email your veterinarian and explain the problem. He or she can then advise you if the problem requires an office visit or not.

However, you must always seek prompt veterinary care if your pet exhibits any of the following signs or symptoms:

- Traumatic injuries, such as lacerations, burns, broken bones, cracked shells or puncture wounds

- Sores, ulcers, lumps or other deformations of the skin

- Intestinal disturbances that do not resolve within 48 hours

- Drastic change in behavior

- Inability to deposit eggs

Remember that reptiles are perfectly capable of feeling pain and suffering, so apply the golden rule: If you would appreciate medical care for an injury or illness, it is likely that your pet does as well.

Common Health Problems

The following are some of the most common health problems that afflict turtles. Be alert for any signs of the following maladies, and take steps to remedy the problem.

Respiratory Infections

Respiratory infections are some of the most common illnesses that afflict turtles and other captive reptiles.

The most common symptoms of respiratory infections are discharges from the nose or mouth; however, lethargy, inappetence and behavioral changes (such as basking more often than normal) may also accompany respiratory infections.

Myriad causes can lead to this type of illness, including communicable pathogens, as well as, ubiquitous, yet normally harmless, pathogens, which opportunistically infect stressed animals.

Your turtle may be able to fight off these infections without veterinary assistance, but it is wise to solicit your vet's opinion at the first sign of illness. Some respiratory infections can prove fatal and require immediate attention.

Your vet will likely obtain samples, send of the samples for laboratory testing and then interpret the results. Antibiotics or other medications may be prescribed to help your turtle recover, and your veterinarian will likely encourage you to keep the turtle's stress level low, and ensure his enclosure temperatures are ideal.

In fact, it is usually a good idea to raise the temperature of the basking spot upon first suspecting that your turtle is suffering from a respiratory infection. Elevated body temperatures (such as those that occur when mammals have fevers) help the turtle's body to fight the infection, and many will bask for longer than normal when ill.

Metabolic Bone Disease

Metabolic bone disease (MBD) is a complicated phenomenon that befalls turtles who are provided with insufficient calcium or insufficient amounts of the active form of vitamin D (D3), which is necessary for calcium utilization.

A well-rounded, diverse diet with plenty of grasses and weeds helps to ensure your pet receives enough calcium. Additionally, many keepers supplement their turtle's food items with calcium powders. However, it is important to consult with your veterinarian to devise a suitable supplementation schedule, as providing too much calcium can be just as problematic as providing too little.

A balanced diet will provide your turtle with plenty of inactive vitamin D. To allow your pet to convert this into the active form, you must provide it with exposure to ultraviolet radiation (specifically UVB). This can be accomplished either by housing your turtle outdoors and allowing them to bask in natural sunlight, or by illuminating their enclosure with full spectrum lights that produce light in the UVB portion of the spectrum.

When deprived of proper lighting, the calcium levels in the turtle's blood fall. This causes the turtle's body to draw calcium from the bones (including the shell) to rectify the problem.

As calcium is removed from the bones, they become soft and flexible, rather than hard and rigid. This can lead to broken bones or disfigurement, which can leave your turtle unable to eat, walk or swim.

Advanced cases of MBD are rarely treatable, and euthanasia is often the only humane option. However, when caught early and treated aggressively, some of the symptoms of the disease can be stopped. Accordingly, it is of the upmost importance to seek veterinary care at the first sign of MBD.

Shell Rot

Shell rot is a catchall term for a variety of maladies related to a turtle's shell. Shell rot normally takes the form of lesions or ulcers; sometimes, a small amount of fluid may leak from the wounds.

Shell rot may occur because of a systematic infection or as a local phenomenon. Bacteria or fungi may be the primary cause of the problem, or injuries may provide an opportunity for pathogens to colonize the tissues.

Shell rot is usually treatable with prompt veterinary care, so always see your veterinarian at the first sign of problems.

Parasites

Parasites are rare among captive-bred turtles, but poor husbandry can cause them to become a problem. Parasites rarely become problematic for wild turtles, unless they become injured, stressed or ill.

Most internal parasites cause intestinal problems, such as runny or watery stools, vomiting or decreased appetites. Your veterinarian can collect blood or stool samples from your turtle, analyze them to determine what parasites, if any, are present, and prescribe medications to clear the infestation. Often, multiple treatments are necessary to eradicate the parasites completely.

External parasites afflict turtles on occasion, usually in the form of leeches. Have your veterinarian assist you in removing any leeches present to help reduce the possibility of infection.

Anorexia

Mata matas are normally ravenous eaters, who rarely pass up the chance to consume calories. However, they may refuse food if ill, if kept in suboptimal temperatures (including seasonally cool temperatures, such as occur during the winter) or are preoccupied by breeding.

Refusing a meal or two is not cause for alarm, but if your turtle refuses food for longer than this, be sure to review your husbandry practices. If the turtle continues to refuse food without an obvious reason for doing so, consult your veterinarian.

Injuries

Despite their protective shells and armored legs, mata matas can become injured in myriad ways, including battles with cagemates, overly zealous breeding attempts, or by sustaining burns from heaters. While turtles are likely to heal from most minor wounds without medical attention, serious wounds will necessitate veterinary assistance.

Your vet will likely clean the wound, make any repairs necessary (shell patches, sutures, etc.) and prescribe a course of antibiotics to help prevent infection. Be sure to keep the enclosure as clean as possible during the healing process.

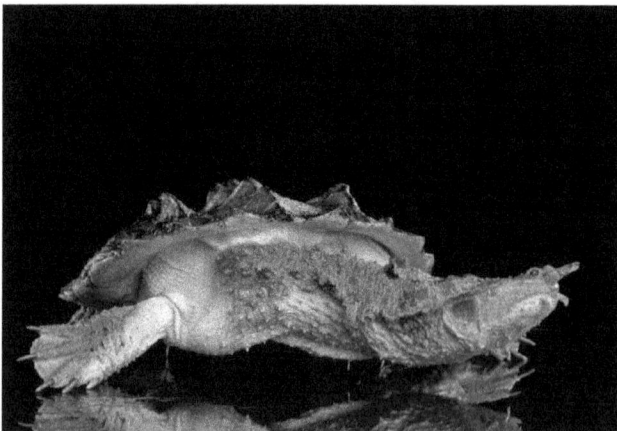

Be sure to examine all of the skin folds on your turtle regularly.

Egg Binding

Egg binding occurs when a female is unable or unwilling to deposit her eggs in a timely fashion. If not treated promptly, death can result.

The primary symptoms of egg binding are similar to those that occur when a gravid turtle approaches parturition. Egg bound turtles may dig to create an egg chamber or attempt to escape their enclosure. However, unlike turtles who will deposit eggs normally, egg bound turtles continue to exhibit these symptoms without producing a clutch of eggs.

As long as you are expecting your turtle to lay eggs, you can easily monitor her behavior and act quickly if she experiences problems. However, if you are not anticipating a clutch, this type of problem can catch you by surprise.

Prolapse

Prolapses occur when a turtle's intestines protrude from its vent. This is an emergency situation that requires prompt treatment. Fortunately, intestinal prolapse is not terribly common among turtles.

You will need to take the animal to the veterinarian, who will attempt to re-insert the intestinal sections. Sometimes sutures will be necessary to keep the intestines in place while the muscles regain their tone.

Try to keep the exposed tissue damp, clean and protected while traveling to the vet. It is likely that this problem is very painful for the animal, so try to keep its stress level low during the process.

Quarantine

Quarantine is the practice of isolating animals to prevent them from transferring diseases between themselves.

If you have no other pet reptiles (particularly turtles), quarantine is unnecessary. However, if you already maintain other turtles you must provide all new acquisitions with a separate enclosure.

At a minimum, quarantine all new acquisitions for 30 days. However, it is wiser still to extend the quarantine period for 60 to 90 days, to give yourself a better chance of discovering any illness present before exposing your colony to new, potentially sick, animals. Professional zoological institutions often quarantine animals for six months to a year. In fact, some zoos keep their animals in a state of perpetual quarantine.

Chapter 15: Mata Mata Turtles

Many – if not most – turtle keepers are eventually bitten by the captive breeding bug. Determined to produce a clutch of adorable hatchlings, these keepers acquire specimens of each sex and begin waiting for eggs.

This is a natural progression for keepers, and, when carried out in responsible fashion, breeding can be beneficial for the species, as captive breeding projects help alleviate pressure on wild populations.

However, irresponsible breeders often cause serious problems for the hobby.

Such breeders often set out with the explicit goal of profiting from their turtles, rather than enjoying their pets in their own right. This ensures failure for the vast majority of people that try to breed turtles for profit.

It is also important to point out that mata matas are not bred with great frequency. The turtles are challenging to maintain, and achieving captive reproduction is even more difficult. Also, as fairly large animals, it is difficult to provide accommodations big enough for a pair of mata matas.

This doesn't mean that well-intentioned and prepared keepers shouldn't attempt to breed mata matas. To the contrary, increased captive breeding efforts would help take pressure of wild populations. But, you should undertake such endeavors with the understanding that you may not ever succeed.

Given the infrequency with which these turtles are bred, it should come as no surprise that a precise "formula" for breeding them has been devised yet.

Accordingly, you may find it necessary to experiment heavily, by manipulating the photoperiod, temperatures and social factors within the enclosure to achieve success.

Pre-Breeding Considerations

Before you set out to breed mata matas, consider the decision carefully. Unfortunately, few keepers realize the implications of breeding their turtles before they set out to do so.

Ask yourself if you will be able to:

- Provide adequate care for a pair of adult turtles
- Provide the proper care for the female while gravid
- Afford emergency veterinary services if necessary
- Incubate the eggs in some type of incubator
- Provide housing for the hatchlings
- Provide food for the hatchlings
- Dedicate the time to caring for the hatchlings
- Find new homes for the hatchlings

If you cannot answer each of these questions affirmatively, you are not in a position to breed painted turtles responsibly.

Legal Issues

Before deciding to breed turtles, you must investigate the relevant laws in your area. Some municipalities require turtle breeders to obtain licenses, insurance and permits, although others do not.

Finally, be aware that it is illegal to buy or sell turtles with carapaces less than 4 inches in length in the United States, except for educational or scientific purposes. This is a particularly important consideration when breeding relatively small turtles, because you may need to house them for some time, while waiting for them to attain the minimum size necessary.

Sexing Mata Mata Turtles

If, after considering the proposition carefully, you decide to breed mata matas, you will need at least one sexual pair of animals. To be sure that you have a sexed pair, you must be able to distinguish one sex from the other.

While it is difficult to identify the sex of young mata matas, it is relatively easy to distinguish between the sexes by the time they are mature.

The best way to distinguish the sex of these turtles is by examining their tails. Males also have longer, thicker tails than females do, and the vent is usually positioned more distally than it is in females. Females may reach slightly larger sizes than males too, but this is not a good criteria for distinguishing the sexes.

Pre-Breeding Conditioning

Once you have obtained a sexual pair, you must begin conditioning them for breeding. This is important because animals that are not in very good condition may not be able to handle the rigors of cycling and breeding.

Take the turtles to visit your veterinarian, who will be able to ascertain their health status. Some veterinarians may only perform a visual inspection, but others may collect biological samples for additional testing.

If your vet determines that your turtles are not healthy, take whatever steps are recommended to rectify the problem before commencing breeding trials.

Once you are certain that your turtles are in good health, it is time to initiate your breeding protocols.

Cycling

Cycling is a term used to describe the practice of providing captive reptiles with an annual variation in temperature (or other factors, such as photoperiod). The concept seeks to mimic the natural seasonal cycle and synchronize the reproductive cycle of the reptiles in question.

However, the proper cycling regimen has yet to be established for mata matas. Cycling may not even be necessary to breed these turtles who hail from tropical climates.

Groupings and Housing

Some keepers prefer to keep the sexes separate for most of the year, and only introduce them to each other during breeding trials. Others maintain their animals together throughout the year.

While both of these approaches are valid for most turtle species, it is not a good idea for these turtles. Mata matas do not normally interact outside of the breeding season, and they may be antagonistic to any other animals that share their habitat.

So, most keepers maintain their mata matas separately for the bulk of the year, and only introduce them to the same cage for brief mating attempts.

Gravid

Shortly after successful copulation, suitably healthy females become gravid. Unlike many other reptiles, turtles do not offer very many signs to indicate their reproductive condition.

Manual palpation, which is a common method for determining the reproductive condition of many other reptiles, is rarely helpful with turtles. In fact, attempting to feel a female's eggs with your fingers may cause them to rupture. Accordingly, it is wise to avoid the practice entirely. Instead, the best clues lie in the female's behavior.

Gravid turtles may bask for longer periods of time, and begin eating very little food as their eggs develop and take up more space in their body cavity. They may also begin to explore their surroundings and look for a suitable place to dig their eggs.

Nevertheless, the only way to be certain that your turtle is gravid is by having your veterinarian perform an x-ray. This will not only verify that she is holding eggs, but it will allow you to know approximately how many eggs she is carrying.

Egg Deposition

As the time for egg deposition nears, the female will become increasingly restless. She may pace for long periods of time or even look for a way to escape from the enclosure.

At this point, the female is seeking out a place to dig a nest and deposit her eggs. Hopefully, you have designed the enclosure so that such a place is always available, but, if you have not, you must provide her with a place she finds suitable.

Typically, mata matas look for a place that is close to the water and allows them to dig easily. Ideally, the egg-deposition site should have a footprint of at least two to three times the size of the turtle's shell and contain substrate as deep as the turtle's shell is long.

If your female does not find the provided site to her liking, you will need to tweak it until she feels comfortable. This can mean loosening the substrate, compacting the substrate, providing a greater depth of substrate or moving the egg deposition site to another location in the enclosure.

This is often a challenging component of turtle breeding, and even highly experienced zookeepers occasionally have problems devising a suitable egg-laying site.

If your turtle cannot find a suitable place to lay her eggs, she may scatter the eggs in the enclosure or retain them internally. Usually, these outcomes lead to health problems for the female, such as dystocia (egg binding).

Assuming that your turtle finds the egg deposition area suitable, she will eventually crawl into it, dig a small depression and fill it with about 10 to 25 eggs. After completing the process, she will cover the hole and leave the area. It can be very difficult to locate a nest site afterwards, so do your best to mark the location during, or immediately after, parturition.

Egg Incubation

Keepers employ any of several different strategies for incubating mata mata eggs. No one method is "correct," although artificially incubating the eggs in a climate-controlled container usually leads to the greatest success.

To do so, you'll need to excavate the egg chamber, remove the eggs and place them in a climate-controlled incubator for the remainder of their development.

Use great care when excavating the egg chamber to prevent damaging the eggs. Once you have accessed the eggs, mark the top of each with a graphite pencil. This will allow you to maintain the correct orientation when transferring the eggs to the incubator; inverting the eggs can cause the embryos to drown.

Avoid separating any eggs that have adhered to each other. While it is often possible to do so without damaging the eggs, such attempts should be left to those who have considerable experience incubating reptile eggs.

Egg Boxes

Egg boxes are small plastic storage boxes designed to hold the eggs inside the incubator. While their use is not always necessary in the strictest sense, they make it easier to maintain the climate surrounding the eggs.

Virtually any type of small plastic storage box will suffice, but consider a few things before selecting your egg boxes:

1. Be sure to select boxes that are tall enough to contain 1 or 2 inches (2.5 to 5 centimeters) of incubation media as well as the eggs, which will rest on top of the media (partially buried).
2. Whenever possible, select transparent egg boxes so that you can observe the eggs without having to open them.
3. If possible, select boxes with domed lids, which will help prevent condensation from dripping on the eggs.

You will need to make two small holes (approximately one-quarter-inch or one-half centimeter in diameter) in each box to allow for air exchange inside the egg boxes.

Some breeders prefer to monitor the temperature of the egg boxes, while others prefer to monitor the temperature of the incubator. Either method will work, although if you desire to measure the temperatures inside the egg boxes, you will need to drill additional holes to accept a temperature probe.

You can select relatively large egg boxes so that they will accommodate large clutches, or you can use relatively small egg boxes, so that you can split up the clutch into several different sub groups.

Incubation Media

Several different incubation media are appropriate for egg incubation. Soil, soil and sand mixtures and vermiculite are some of the most common choices by breeders. Vermiculite works for a wide variety of reptile eggs, as it is quite easy to attain a suitable moisture level.

The substrate not only provides a protective cushion that supports the eggs, but it also provides moisture, which will keep the relative humidity of the egg box high. This will prevent the eggs from desiccating.

Too much humidity or dampness, however, can have a negative effect on the eggs, so it is important to keep enough water in the egg boxes, but not too much.

Many keepers strive to maintain humidity levels of 80 to 90 percent in the egg chamber, but others simply watch the eggs and adjust the humidity accordingly. If the eggs begin to exhibit wrinkles, they are drying out and more water is necessary. Conversely, if they begin to swell or exude fluid, the humidity should be lowered.

Some authorities recommend specific ratios of water and vermiculite, but as vermiculite absorbs water from the air, it is impossible to know how saturated the vermiculite was when you started.

Accordingly, the best approach is to judge the moisture with your hands. Beginning with dry vermiculite, slowly add water while stirring the mixture. The goal is to dampen the vermiculite just enough that it clumps when compressed in your hand. However, if water drips from the media when you squeeze it, the vermiculite is too damp.

The Incubator

You can either purchase a commercially produced incubator or construct your own. However, most beginning breeders are better served by purchasing a commercial incubator than making their own.

Commercial Incubators

Commercial egg incubators come in myriad styles and sizes. Some of the most popular models are similar to those used to incubate poultry eggs (these are often available for purchase from livestock supply retailers).

These incubators are constructed from a large foam box, fitted with a heating element and thermostat. Some models feature a fan for circulating air; while helpful for maintaining a uniform thermal environment, models that lack these fans are acceptable.

You can place an incubation medium directly in the bottom of these types of incubators, although it is preferable to place the media (and eggs) inside small plastic storage boxes, which are then placed inside the incubator.

These incubators are usually affordable and easy to use, although their foam-based construction makes them less durable than most premium incubators are.

Other incubators are constructed from metal or plastic boxes; feature a clear door, an enclosed heating element and a thermostat. Some units also feature a backup thermostat, which can provide some additional protection in case the primary thermostat fails.

These types of incubators usually outperform economy, foam-based models, but they also bear higher price tags. Either style will work, but, if you plan to breed turtles for many years, premium models usually present the best option.

Homemade Incubators

Although incubators can be constructed in a variety of ways, using many different materials and designs, two basic designs are most common.

The first type of homemade incubator consists of a plastic, glass or wood box, and a simple heat source, such as a piece of heat tape or a low-wattage heat lamp. The heating source must be attached to a thermostat to keep the temperatures consistent. A thermometer is also necessary for monitoring the temperatures of the incubator.

Some keepers make these types of incubators from wood, while others prefer plastic or foam. Although glass is a poor insulator, aquariums often serve as acceptable incubators; however, you must purchase or construct a solid top to retain heat.

Place a brick on the bottom of the incubator, and place the egg box on top of the brick, so that the eggs are not resting directly on the heat tape. The brick will also provide thermal mass to the incubator, which will help maintain a more consistent temperature.

The other popular incubator design adds a quantity of water to the design to help maintain consistent temperatures and a higher humidity. To build such a unit, begin with an aquarium fitted with a glass or plastic lid.

Place a brick in the bottom of the aquarium and add about two gallons of water to the aquarium; ideally, the water level should stop right below the top of the brick.

Add an aquarium heater to the water and set the thermostat to the desired temperature. Place the egg box on the brick, insert a temperature probe into the egg box and cover the aquarium with the lid (you may need to purchase a lid designed to allow the cords to pass through it).

This type of incubator works by heating the water, which will in turn heat the air inside the incubator, which will heat the eggs. Although it can take several days of repeated adjustments to get these types of incubators set to the exact temperature you would like, they are very stable once established.

Incubation Temperature and Duration

As with the adult animals, the biological processes taking place inside reptile eggs are determined by the temperature at which they are kept. The warmer the environment is, the quicker the eggs develop; the cooler the environment is, the longer it takes the eggs to complete their development.

This basic principle likely holds true for mata matas. However, this does not mean that their eggs can be incubated at any temperature – in fact, the ideal temperature for incubating the eggs of these turtles is not known. But, eggs kept below the minimum acceptable temperature will fail to live, just as those kept above the maximum acceptable temperature will.

A good temperature range for mata mata egg incubation is probably between about 79 and 86 degrees Fahrenheit (approximately 26 to 30 degrees Celsius).

Depending on the temperature of your home – you may be able to incubate the eggs at "room temperature."

However, doing so will invariably expose the eggs to temperature fluctuations. Minor temperature fluctuations are not harmful to the eggs, but massive swings in temperature predispose the eggs to failure or cause the young to be abnormal.

The duration of the incubation period is about 200 days. However, individuals develop at slightly different speeds, so the young may hatch over a period of days. In some cases, the first and last hatchling to emerge from the eggs may be separated by a week's time.

Neonatal Husbandry

Observe the hatchlings as they emerge from their shells. Some turtles will remain in their shells for several days while they absorb the rest of their egg yolk. This is perfectly normal, and you should NOT remove such turtles from their eggs. Allow the turtle to absorb the entire yolk and exit the egg on his own.

If for some reason, the egg becomes destroyed (such as through the activities of the clutchmates), move the turtle into a clean, plastic container with about 1/4 inch of water in the bottom. Do not pull the yolk free, and try to keep it from drying out.

Once the turtles have hatched and absorbed their egg yolk, they are ready to move to the nursery. The nursery container should be constructed from a small plastic storage box (you can split the clutch among several different boxes to reduce the stress on the hatchlings).

Drill or melt a few small ventilation holes in the top (always making sure the holes are drilled from the inside toward the outside to prevent any sharp edges from injuring the hatchlings) and place enough water in the bottom to cover the hatchlings' shells.

Leave the hatchlings inside the nursery for at least 24 hours to ensure they have absorbed their egg yolks are have become active.

Once a turtle has become active, you can move it to its "permanent" home. You can house a few hatchlings together in the same habitat, but it is preferable to house them singly.

You can begin feeding them almost immediately after placing them in their new homes, but many will not begin feeding for a few days.

Chapter 16: Further Reading

Never stop learning more about your new pet's natural history, biology and captive care. This is the only way to ensure that you are providing your new turtle with the highest quality of life possible.

It's always more fun to watch your turtle than it is to read about him, but by accumulating more knowledge, you'll be better able to provide him with a high quality of life.

Books

Bookstores and online book retailers offer a treasure trove of information that will advance your quest for knowledge. While books represent an additional cost involved in reptile care, you can consider it an investment in your pet's well-being. Your local library may also carry some books about mata matas, which you can borrow for no charge.

University libraries are a great place for finding old, obscure or academically oriented books about turtles. You may not be allowed to borrow these books if you are not a student, but you can view and read them at the library.

Herpetology: An Introductory Biology of Amphibians and Reptiles
By Laurie J. Vitt, Janalee P. Caldwell
Academic Press, 2013

Understanding Reptile Parasites: A Basic Manual for Herpetoculturists & Veterinarians
By Roger Klingenberg D.V.M.
Advanced Vivarium Systems, 1997

Infectious Diseases and Pathology of Reptiles: Color Atlas and Text
Elliott Jacobson
CRC Press

Designer Reptiles and Amphibians
Richard D. Bartlett, Patricia Bartlett
Barron's Educational Series

Magazines

Because magazines are typically published monthly or bi-monthly, they occasionally offer more up-to-date information than books do. Magazine articles are obviously not as comprehensive as books typically are, but they still have considerable value.

Reptiles Magazine
www.reptilesmagazine.com/
Covering reptiles commonly kept in captivity.

Practical Reptile Keeping
http://www.practicalreptilekeeping.co.uk/
Practical Reptile Keeping is a popular publication aimed at beginning and advanced hobbies. Topics include the care and maintenance of popular reptiles as well as information on wild reptiles.

Websites

The internet has made it much easier to find information about reptiles than it has ever been.

However, you must use discretion when deciding which websites to trust. While knowledgeable breeders, keepers and academics operate some websites, many who maintain reptile-oriented websites lack the same dedication to scientific rigor.

Anyone with a computer and internet connection can launch a website and say virtually anything they want about turtles. Accordingly, as with all other research, consider the source of the information before making any husbandry decisions.

The Reptile Report

www.thereptilereport.com/

The Reptile Report is a news-aggregating website that accumulates interesting stories and features about reptiles from around the world.

Kingsnake.com

www.kingsnake.com

After starting as a small website for gray-banded kingsnake enthusiasts, Kingsnake.com has become one of the largest reptile-oriented portals in the hobby. The site features classified advertisements, a breeder directory, message forums and other resources.

The Vivarium and Aquarium News

www.vivariumnews.com/

The online version of the former print publication, The Vivarium and Aquarium News provides in-depth coverage of different reptiles and amphibians in a captive and wild context.

Journals

Journals are the primary place professional scientists turn when they need to learn about turtles. While they may not make light reading, hobbyists stand to learn a great deal from journals.

Herpetologica

www.hljournals.org/

Published by The Herpetologists' League, Herpetologica, and its companion publication, Herpetological Monographs cover all aspects of reptile and amphibian research.

Journal of Herpetology
www.ssarherps.org/
Produced by the Society for the Study of Reptiles and Amphibians, the Journal of Herpetology is a peer-reviewed publication covering a variety of reptile-related topics.

Copeia
www.asihcopeiaonline.org/
Copeia is published by the American Society of Ichthyologists and Herpetologists. A peer-reviewed journal, Copeia covers all aspects of the biology of reptiles, amphibians and fish.

Nature
www.nature.com/
Although Nature covers all aspects of the natural world, many issues contain information that turtle enthusiasts are sure to find interesting.

Supplies
You can obtain most of what you need to mata matas through your local pet store, big-box retailer or hardware store, but online retailers offer another option.

Just be sure that you consider the shipping costs for any purchase, to ensure you aren't "saving" yourself a few dollars on the product, yet spending several more dollars to get the product delivered.

Big Apple Pet Supply
http://www.bigappleherp.com

Big Apple Pet Supply carries most common husbandry equipment, including heating devices, water dishes and substrates.

LLLReptile
http://www.lllreptile.com
LLL Reptile carries a wide variety of husbandry tools, heating devices, lighting products and more.

Doctors Foster and Smith
http://www.drsfostersmith.com
Foster and Smith is a veterinarian-owned retailer that supplies husbandry-related items to pet keepers.

Support Organizations
Sometimes, the best way to learn about turtles is to reach out to other keepers and breeders. Check out these organizations, and search for others in your geographic area.

The National Reptile & Amphibian Advisory Council
http://www.nraac.org/
The National Reptile & Amphibian Advisory Council seeks to educate the hobbyists, legislators and the public about reptile and amphibian related issues.

American Veterinary Medical Association
www.avma.org
The AVMA is a good place for Americans to turn if you are having trouble finding a suitable reptile veterinarian.

The World Veterinary Association
http://www.worldvet.org/
The World Veterinary Association is a good resource for finding suitable reptile veterinarians worldwide.

References

Anderson, S. P. (2003). The Phylogenetic Definition of Reptilia. *Systematic Biology*.

Crawford, N. G. (2012). A phylogenomic analysis of turtles. *Molecular Phylogenetics and Evolution*.

Khalil, F. (1947). Excretion in Reptiles. *Journal of Biological Chemisty*.

Patrick Lemell, C. L. (2002). Feeding patterns of Chelus fimbriatus (Pleurodira: Chelidae). *Journal of Experimental Biology*.

Patrick Lemell, C. L. (2010). The feeding apparatus of Chelus fimbriatus (Pleurodira; Chelidae) – adaptation perfected? *Ampibia-Reptilia* .

Pritchard, P. C. (2008). Chelus Fimbriata -- Matamata turtle. *Conservation Biology of Freshwater Turtles and Tortoises*.

Winokur, R. M. (1982). Integumentary appendages of chelonians. *Journal of Morphology*.